COMPANIONS FC

MW01029710

Praying with Faustina

Eileen Dunn Bertanzetti

the WORD among us® press

Published by The Word Among Us Press, 9639 Doctor Perry Road
Ijamsville, Maryland 21754
www.wordamongus.org

12 11 10 09 08   1 2 3 4 5
ISBN: 978-1-59325-135-2

Cover design by The DesignWorks Group

Made and printed in the United States of America

Library of Congress Cataloging-in-Publication Data
Bertanzetti, Eileen Dunn.
Praying with Faustina / Eileen Dunn Bertanzetti.
p. cm.
ISBN 978-1-59325-135-2
1. Meditations. 2. Faustina, Saint, 1905-1938--Prayers and devotions.
I. Title.
BV4832.3.B48 2008
242--dc22

2008002902

Contents

Foreword

Companions for the Journey

Just as food is required for human life, so are companions. Indeed, the word "companion" comes from two Latin words: *com,* meaning "with," and *panis,* meaning "bread." Companions nourish our heart, mind, soul, and body. They are also the people with whom we can celebrate the sharing of bread.

Perhaps the most touching stories in the Bible are about companionship: the Last Supper, the wedding feast at Cana, the sharing of the loaves and the fishes, and Jesus' breaking bread with the disciples on the road to Emmaus. Each incident of companionship with Jesus revealed more about his mercy, love, wisdom, suffering, and hope. When Jesus went to pray in the Garden of Gethsemane, he craved the companionship of the apostles. They let him down. But God sent the Spirit to inflame the hearts of the apostles, and they became faithful companions to Jesus and to each other.

Throughout history, other faithful companions have followed Jesus and the apostles. These saints and mystics have also taken the journey from conversion, through suffering, to resurrection. Just as they were inspired by the holy people who went before them, so too may you take them as your companions as you walk on your spiritual journey.

The Companions for the Journey series is a response to the spiritual hunger of Christians. This series makes available the rich spiritual teachings of mystics and guides whose wisdom can help us on our pilgrimage. Our hope is that, as you complete each meditation, you will feel supported, challenged, and affirmed by a soul companion on your spiritual journey.

The spiritual hunger that has emerged in the last few decades is a great sign of renewal in Christian life. People fill retreat programs and workshops on topics in spirituality. The demand for spiritual directors exceeds the number available. Interest in the lives and writings of saints and mystics is increasing as people search for models of whole and holy Christian life.

Praying with the Saints

Praying with Faustina is more than just a book about Faustina's spirituality. This book seeks to engage you in praying in the way that St. Faustina did about issues and themes that were central to her experience. Each meditation can enlighten your understanding of her revelations and lead you to reflect on your own experience.

The goal of *Praying with Faustina* is that you will discover her wonderfully alive spirituality and integrate her spirit and wisdom into your relationship with God, with your brothers and sisters, and with your own heart and mind.

Suggestions for Praying with Faustina

Meet Faustina, a caring companion for your pilgrimage, by reading the Introduction, which begins on page 13. It provides a brief biography and the major themes of her spirituality.

Once you meet Faustina, you will be ready to pray with her and to encounter God, your human sisters and brothers, and yourself in new and wonderful ways. To help your prayer, here are some suggestions that have been part of the tradition of Christian spirituality:

Create a sacred space. Jesus said, "Whenever you pray, go into your room and shut the door and pray to your Father who is in secret; and your Father who sees in secret will reward you" (Matthew 6:6). Solitary prayer is best done in a place where you can have privacy and silence, both of which can be luxuries in the lives of busy people. If privacy and silence are not possible, create a quiet, safe place within yourself, perhaps while riding to and from work, while waiting in the dentist's office, or while waiting for someone. Do the best you can, knowing that a loving God is present everywhere. Whether the meditations in this book are used for solitary prayer or with a group, try to create a prayerful mood with candles, meditative music, a crucifix, or an image of Mary.

Open yourself to the power of prayer. Every human experience has a religious dimension. All of life is suffused with God's presence. So remind yourself that God is present as you begin your period of prayer. Do not worry about distractions. If something keeps intruding during your prayer, spend some time talking with God about it. Be flexible, because God's Spirit blows where it will.

Prayer can open your mind and widen your vision. Be open to new ways of seeing God, people, and yourself. As you open yourself to the Spirit of God, different emotions are evoked, such as sadness from tender memories or joy from a celebration recalled. Our emotions are messages from God that can tell us much about our spiritual quest. Also, prayer strengthens our will to act. Through prayer, God can touch our will and empower us to live according to what we know is true.

Finally, many of the meditations in this book will call you to employ your memories, your imagination, and the circumstances of your life as subjects for prayer. The great mystics and saints realized that they had to use all of their resources to know God better. Indeed, God speaks to us continually and touches us constantly. We must learn to listen and feel with all the means that God has given us.

Come to prayer with an open mind, heart, and will.

Preview each meditation before beginning. Spend a few moments previewing the readings and especially the reflection activities. Several reflection activities are given in each meditation, because different styles of prayer appeal to different personalities or personal needs. *Note that each meditation has more reflection activities than can be done during one prayer period. Therefore, select only one or two reflection activities each time you use a meditation. Do not feel compelled to complete all of the reflection activities.*

Read meditatively. After you have placed yourself in God's presence, the meditations offer you a story about Faustina and a selection from her writings. Take your time reading. If a particular phrase touches you, stay with it. Relish its feelings, meanings, and concerns.

Use the reflections. Following "Faustina's Words" is a short reflection in commentary form, meant to give perspective to the readings. Then you will be offered several ways of meditating on the readings and the theme of the prayer. You may be familiar with the different methods of meditating, but in case you are not, they are described briefly here:

- Repeated centering prayer: One means of focusing your prayer is to use a centering prayer. The prayer may be a single word or a short phrase taken from the readings or from the Scriptures. For example, a centering prayer for a meditation on courage might be "I go before you" or "trust." Repeated slowly in harmony with your breathing, the prayer helps you center your heart and mind on one action or attribute of God.

- *Lectio divina:* This type of meditation is "divine studying," a concentrated reflection on the word of God or the wisdom of a spiritual writer. Most often in *lectio divina,* you will be invited to read one of the passages several times and then concentrate on one or two sentences, pondering their meaning for you and their effect on you. *Lectio divina* commonly ends with the formulation of a resolution.

- Guided meditation: In this type of meditation, our imagination helps us consider alternative actions and likely consequences. Our imagination helps us experience new ways of seeing God, our neighbors, ourselves, and nature. When Jesus told his followers parables and stories, he engaged their imagination. In this book, you will be asked to follow a guided meditation.

  One way of doing a guided meditation is to read the scene or story several times until you know the outline and can recall it when you enter into reflection. Or before your prayer time, you may wish to record the meditation on a tape recorder. If so, remember to allow pauses for reflection between phrases and to speak with a slow, peaceful pace and tone. Then during prayer, when you have finished the readings and the reflection commentary, you can turn on your recording of the meditation and be led through it. If you find your own voice too distracting, ask a friend to make the tape for you.

- Examen of consciousness: The reflections often will ask you to examine how God has been speaking to you in your past and present experience—in other words, the reflections will ask you to examine your awareness of God's presence in your life.

- Journal writing: Writing is a process of discovery. If you write for any length of time, stating honestly what is on your mind and in your heart, you will unearth much about who you are, how you stand with your God, what deep longings reside in your soul, and more. In some of the reflections, you may be asked to write a dialogue with Jesus or someone else. If you have never used writing as a means of meditation, try it. Reserve a special notebook for your journal writing. If desired, you can go back to your entries at a future time for an examen of consciousness.

- Action: Occasionally, a reflection may suggest singing a favorite hymn, going out for a walk, or undertaking some other physical activity. Actions can be meaningful forms of prayer.

Using the Meditations for Group or Family Prayer

If you wish to use the meditations for community prayer, these suggestions may be of help:

- Read the theme to the group. Call the group into the presence of God, using the short opening prayer. Invite one or two participants to read one or both of the readings. If you use both readings, observe the pause between them.

- You may decide to use the reflection as a reading or to skip it, depending on the needs and interests of the group.

- Select one of the reflection activities for your group. Allow sufficient time for your group to reflect, to say a centering prayer, to accomplish a studying prayer (*lectio divina*), or to finish an examen of consciousness. Depending on the group and the amount of time available, you may want to invite the participants to share their reflections, responses, or petitions with the group.

- Reading the passage from the Scriptures may serve as a summary of the meditation.

- If a formulated prayer or a psalm is given as a closing, it may be recited by the entire group. Or you may ask participants to offer their own prayers for the closing.

Now you are ready to pray with Faustina, a compassionate and challenging companion on your spiritual journey. May you find her to be a true companion for your soul.

Introduction

On October 5, 1938, in the isolation ward in a convent in Krakow, Poland, thirty-three-year-old Sr. Maria Faustina of the Most Blessed Sacrament died after years of suffering from tuberculosis. Except for her family, confessors, spiritual director, and fellow nuns, few knew her. And only a few priests and superiors at the half-dozen Sisters of Our Lady of Mercy convents at which Faustina lived and worked knew of the mission Jesus had entrusted to her: to tell the world about Jesus' limitless mercy, to practice mercy, and to beg God to have mercy on all.

In a vision to Sr. Faustina, Jesus manifested himself as the Divine Mercy. Calling her his "Secretary,"[1] he asked her to write down everything he would tell her concerning his unfathomable love and mercy. The result was her handwritten diary, now the equivalent of six hundred printed pages, which has been translated into numerous languages and distributed throughout the world. In her diary, Faustina encourages us to have no fear in approaching Jesus, because our loving Lord desires to forgive us. Jesus told Faustina that even the worst sinner has a *right* to his mercy.

Shortly before Faustina's death in 1938, Christ's message of mercy and the Divine Mercy image appeared in thousands of small pamphlets. On September 1, 1939, Germany invaded Poland, launching World War II. During that time, those small pamphlets of hope were carried all over the country and eventually outside of it by Poles trying to escape the horrors of the German occupation and the grim specter of imprisonment in death camps. The Divine Mercy message Jesus had transmitted through Faustina brought comfort and hope to millions throughout the world.

The widespread outpouring of popular veneration of Faustina led to prayers for her intercession. The Church eventually declared that two healings from those prayers were miracles wrought through Faustina's intercession, and on April 20, 2000, Pope John Paul II declared her the first saint of the third millennium. Now, from heaven, as she had promised, St. Maria Faustina Kowalska intercedes to God for all who turn to her, for all who trust God to fulfill their urgent need for Christ's love and mercy.

Faustina's Story

Jezu, Ufam Tobie. "Jesus, I trust in You."[2] Alone on the evening of February 21, 1931, in her convent cell, Sr. Maria Faustina saw Jesus Christ. Wearing a long white garment, he raised one hand, as if bestowing a blessing. The Lord's other hand touched his garment above his heart, and from that area two large rays emanated, one red and one pale, as if translucent. Awed, Faustina gazed at Jesus in silence, her soul filled with joy. He spoke and told her to paint a picture of this vision of him and to write at the bottom of the painting, as if the words were a signature, *Jezu,*

Ufam Tobie (Jesus, I trust in you). He promised Sr. Faustina that he would forever protect anyone who venerated this image.

Early Years

On August 25, 1905, Helena Kowalska was born in her parents' small cottage in the village of Glogowiec, Poland. Surrounded by small farms in an agricultural region close to the heart of foreign-ruled Poland, Glogowiec was home to poor farming people like Helena's parents, Stanislaus and Marianna Kowalski.[3] Before World War II, most of Poland's citizens worked as farmers, although Stanislaus sometimes also worked as a carpenter to support his large family. To help her parents, Helena soon learned how to perform daily chores, including milking the few Kowalski cows. With God as the center of Stanislaus and Marianna Kowalski's lives, Helena also learned from them what it meant to love God.

When she was five, Helena awoke one morning and announced to her family that she had dreamed about the Virgin Mary. Contemplative by nature, the child Helena spent as much time in prayer as she could. This must have perplexed her parents, since none of their other seven surviving children displayed such an extraordinary devotion to God.

When she was six, little Helena felt drawn to an even more intense prayer life, and she would often awaken in the middle of the night to pray. At age seven, she first heard in her soul God's invitation to accept a religious vocation, to live a "more perfect life."[4] Though she had no idea what religious life entailed, even at that young age Helena assented to God's will.

On the morning of her first Communion, just before the onset of the First World War (1914) and in spite of all the talk about war in Poland, Helena joyfully prepared to receive Christ's body and blood. Before she left home that day, she insisted on kissing her parents' hands—an old Polish custom—as a sign of contrition for sins she may have committed and for problems she may have caused them. From then on, before going to confession each week, Helena would ask her parents to forgive her, and then she would kiss their hands. Unlike many children who, after receiving their first Communion, gradually lose their enthusiasm for this greatest of sacraments, Helena's devotion to Jesus' real presence in the Eucharist only grew stronger each day.

During the foreign occupation of Poland, the authorities closed Polish schools. Not until 1917, when she was twelve years old, was Helena allowed to attend school. If it had not been for her father, who years before taught her how to read the Bible and stories about saints and missionaries, she would have entered school illiterate. Instead, the teachers immediately placed her in the second grade.

By the spring of 1919, Helena had successfully completed three winters of schooling. Unfortunately, the authorities decided that the older students, including Helena, had to leave the school in order to make room for younger students. But in spite of her lack of formal education, during her years in the convent as Sr. Faustina, God would use her to write an extensive diary that Pope John Paul II would later declare to be of great significance to all of God's people who sought a deeper spiritual life. Many of today's theologians consider Faustina's *Diary* to be a spiritual classic.

Maid and Babysitter

World War I (1914–1918) brought nationwide suffering, famine, and poverty to Poland. Helena's parents could not even afford to buy each of their daughters a good dress to wear to Sunday Mass, so the Kowalski sisters had to take turns going to Mass and wearing the one good dress they jointly owned. When Helena turned fifteen, she decided to help with the family's finances by getting a job as a maid in a nearby town. Because two of her older sisters had already hired themselves out as housemaids, Helena was able to convince Marianna Kowalska to allow her to also find work outside their home.

Helena excelled as a maid and also took loving care of her employer's little son. But before she had completed a year's work, Helena handed in her resignation. Her reason was that her ever-intensifying prayer had led her to the point where she knew she had to make the decision to enter a convent and lead that "more perfect life" to which Jesus had called her. However, her parents refused to grant their approval. Stanislaus said they had no money for the dowry—the wardrobe she would be required to buy before entering any convent.

Discouraged, Helena worked as a maid and babysitter at several more homes and made several more pleas to her parents for their permission to enter a convent, stating she did not need any money for a wardrobe because Jesus would provide it. Still her parents withheld their permission.

Entrance into Religious Life

Finally, in 1922 Jesus appeared to Helena and asked why she had not yet entered religious life. She knew she could no longer ignore his request. With nothing except the dress she wore and a small bag of essentials, and following Jesus' instructions, Helena took the train to Warsaw. There she obtained a housemaid job at the home of Mrs. Aldona Lipszyc. Helena spent the next several weeks hunting for a convent that would accept her but was turned down at every convent where she applied. Apparently, no one wanted a young woman who had no money, only three winters of schooling, and no significant skills.

One day in 1925, Helena knocked on the door of the Sisters of Our Lady of Mercy motherhouse in Warsaw. When she told the sister doorkeeper she wanted to enter the convent, the nun escorted Helena into the parlor, where she soon met the mother superior, Mother Michael Moraczewska.

Apparently, Helena's humble, amiable personality impressed Mother Michael, because she told the young woman to go to the convent chapel and ask Jesus hidden in the tabernacle if he would accept her. Minutes later when Helena returned to

Mother Michael, she told her that Jesus had indeed accepted her. In turn, the mother superior accepted the Lord's decision and gave Helena permission to join the Sisters of Our Lady of Mercy. However, Helena would have to earn enough money for her convent wardrobe before she could begin her postulancy.

Returning to her employment at the Lipszyc home, Helena worked with joy and gratitude, singing songs of praise and love to God as she cleaned house, cooked, and cared for the children. While Helena's savings for her convent wardrobe gradually accumulated, Mrs. Lipszyc tried to interest her in going out with eligible young men. Gently and kindly Helena refused all the bachelors her employer chose. Helena's heart belonged solely to the Lord of love. But more difficult to bear than Mrs. Lipszyc's matchmaking attempts were Helena's parents' pleas to forsake her plans and return home.

With unwavering determination, Helena stayed at the Lipszyc home, working and saving until she had enough *zlotys* to pay for her required wardrobe. On August 1, 1925, she left the Lipszyc home and hurried to the convent of the Sisters of Our Lady of Mercy. There she gladly handed over her entire savings to the nuns, who warmly welcomed her.

With the Sisters of Our Lady of Mercy

As the sisters welcomed her into their convent, Helena felt as if she had "stepped into the life of Paradise."[5] Yet after only three weeks of convent life as a postulant (which means "one who requests"), Helena believed she had chosen the wrong community of sisters. Their daily schedule did not, in her opinion, allow enough time for prayer. One night she resolved to go to Mother Michael the very next day and tell her of her decision to leave the convent so that she could join a more contemplative religious congregation. Before going to bed, however, Helena stopped in the small chapel of the convent to pray. Instead of obtaining strength of purpose from the Lord to follow through with her decision to leave, she felt a "strange unrest."[6]

When she entered her cell that night, frustrated and uncertain, Helena lay face down on the hard, cold floor and begged God to help her know what he wanted her to do. Moments later a strange brightness filled her cell; she glanced up, and Jesus' grief-stricken, wounded face appeared before her. Helena's loving heart reflected the Lord's pain as she asked him who had hurt him so. Jesus said it was *she* who had caused his pain because she wanted to leave this community of sisters. Helena immediately decided to stay, and peace flooded her heart because she knew that staying was God's will for her.

After completing her postulancy and an eight-day retreat, on April 30, 1926, Helena Kowalska received her habit and took the name Sr. Maria Faustina of the Most Blessed Sacrament. Though she had left her childhood home and the loving Kowalski family, Sr. Faustina now felt as if she had truly come home. She knew she was finally where Jesus wanted her.

Road to Final Vows

From that time until Faustina took her final vows on May 1, 1933, her superiors transferred her multiple times from one congregation house to another, where she worked as a cook, doorkeeper, and gardener. In spite of the frequent moves, perennial ridicule from nuns who failed to understand her spirituality, and serious health problems, including the tuberculosis that would eventually claim her life in 1938, Faustina's spiritual life deepened as she grew ever closer to complete union with God.

By April 28, 1938, Sr. Faustina's physical condition had worsened, and her superiors sent her to a tuberculosis clinic. On her thirty-third birthday, still at the clinic, Faustina received the Sacrament of Anointing of the Sick. On September 17, 1938, she returned home to the Krakow convent to die. Ironically, the same nuns who had spent years ridiculing Faustina now recognized her sanctity and asked her to pray for them when she reached heaven.

On October 5, 1938, Sr. Faustina died in the convent's isolation ward. But the mission Jesus had entrusted to her did not die. After her death, just as she had promised, Faustina began to do more for people than she had done while on earth. And still today, her mission continues as she intercedes for all of us with the God of mercy.

Faustina's Spirituality

In 1934, in obedience to her spiritual director, Msgr. Michael Sopocko, Sr. Faustina began writing a diary in which she recorded the revelations, visions, and mystical experiences given to her by God. In the diary, she also spoke about her spiritual journey, including her insights, prayers, and sufferings. Throughout her short life, she expressed her spirituality through devotion to the Eucharist, Mary, and the Church. She also nurtured a tender devotion to guardian angels, the saints, and the souls in purgatory. Her diary, now the equivalent of six hundred printed pages, also explains the facets of the Divine Mercy Devotion (see Appendix), which Jesus gave to Faustina and asked to have disseminated throughout the world.

Faustina's spirituality is captured in the fifteen meditations included in this book. Here is a short summary of the themes that will be covered:

God Is Love and Mercy

At the core of Faustina's spirituality was her awareness of Christ's invitation to dwell in his merciful love. In return, she was to love him with all her strength and to demonstrate love and mercy to all God's people.

As You Did It to Me: The Corporal Works of Mercy

In her devotion to the divine Redeemer, whom she acknowledged in each individual, Faustina reached out to help anyone who needed her. She served others by doing the seven corporal works of mercy, which include feeding the hungry and giving drink to the thirsty.

Come, O Blessed: The Spiritual Works of Mercy

Faustina found joy in reaching out to help whoever needed her through the spiritual works of mercy, such as praying for the living and the dead and instructing the ignorant.

Mother of Mercy, Your Mother

Faustina knew that the more she loved and imitated the mother of God, the better she came to know and love God himself.

God's Will, Your Daily Food

Sr. Faustina sought to do the holy will of God and called his will her "daily food."[7] She also readily admitted that without God's grace she would never be able to obey him.

Friendship with Jesus

Jesus called Faustina the "apple"[8] of his eye and invited her to accept his divine friendship, which he promised would never end. He said he wants all of us to "snuggle close"[9] to his merciful heart, where we will find peace and joy.

The Most Holy Trinity

Through faith, Sister Faustina experienced God drawing her into his "inner life,"[10] where she was immersed in love and grew to know the Father, Son, and Holy Spirit as one majestic unity, the Holy Trinity.

Road to Sanctification: Suffering

Suffering became prayer for Faustina. She willingly offered all her pain and trials to Jesus. She asked him to unite her sufferings with his for the salvation of souls, as well as for her own sanctification.

To Thee Do I Pray

Faustina learned to remain in God's presence, no matter where she was or what she was doing, and to yield her soul to the Holy Spirit, so that always and everywhere he could pray and intercede through her.

The Most Blessed Sacrament

Faustina frequently meditated before Christ's real presence in the tabernacle. She believed that in holy Communion lay the "whole secret"[11] of her sanctity.

That Heavenly Homeland

Her visions of heaven, purgatory, and hell helped to fuel and form Sr. Faustina's lifelong desire to lead a holy, saintly life and to spend her eternity in that glorious, heavenly homeland to which God has called all people.

Humility

Faustina found that humility was the secret to happiness: knowing that we are totally dependent on God and that we are nothing but "wretchedness and nothingness"[12] without him.

Sharper Than Any Two-Edged Sword

In Scripture Faustina found courage, strength, resolve, and even power to thwart evil and lead a holy life. She knew God's word and applied it to her everyday life.

Interior Silence

Sr. Faustina sought to maintain interior silence at all times, even when performing her assigned chores, so that she could always remain united to and communicating with God who dwelled within her soul.

Jesus, I Trust in You

In her diary, Faustina relates how Jesus wants each of us—everywhere and at all times—to place unwavering trust in him.

Just as St. Thérèse of Lisieux had done, Faustina took a path to sanctity and sainthood that we, too, can follow, because it encompasses nothing spectacular for which the world might praise us. Faustina found God and holiness in faithfully, willingly, and even gratefully performing her daily duties. By accepting as God's will any suffering that entered her life, she allowed him to use that suffering to make her more like her crucified Lord. Her message of God's love and mercy, which penetrated her own soul, is one we still urgently need to hear today, as the late Pope John Paul II made abundantly clear during his pontificate. Along with the pope, let us grasp St. Faustina's hand and travel with her on our spiritual journey, where she will be our guide, prayer partner, and model of sanctity.

1. *Diary of Saint Maria Faustina Kowalska: Divine Mercy in My Soul* (Stockbridge, MA: Marians of the Immaculate Conception, 1987), 1605.

2. *Diary,* 47.

3. Polish masculine surname spellings such as "Kowalski" are used when referring to a male family member or to the entire family, while the feminine, such as "Kowalska," refers only to a female member.

4. *Diary*, 7.

5. *Diary*, 17.

6. *Diary*, 18.

7. *Diary*, 652.

8. *Diary*, 1489.

9. *Diary*, 1074.

10. *Diary*, 734.

11. *Diary*, 1489.

12. *Diary*, 593.

Meditation One

God Is Love and Mercy

Theme: Jesus told Sister Faustina that he is "Love and Mercy."[1] At the core of Faustina's spirituality was her awareness of Christ's invitation to dwell in his merciful love. In return, she was to love him with all her strength and to demonstrate love and mercy to all God's people.

Opening Prayer: Dear Lord, penetrate my heart, mind, and soul with an abiding awareness of your unconditional, merciful love for me. Help me to love you in return, in every circumstance of my life, knowing that my only true joy will be found in loving you and in loving every person because of you.

About Faustina

In 1921, at age sixteen, Helena Kowalska was convinced that God wanted her to lead a "more perfect life,"[2] but she wasn't sure how to do so. In the meantime, she decided to follow in her two older sisters' footsteps and leave home to get a job as a maid. After almost a year living and working in the home of Mrs. Helen Goryszewska, who lived near the large city of Lodz, Helena finally knew what God wanted of her: to enter religious life as a nun. When she mentioned this to her parents, they refused to grant their permission. Out of her great love for God and for them, Helena did not press the issue. Instead, she obtained another job as a live-in maid, this time in the city of Lodz itself.

When autumn 1922 arrived, seventeen-year-old Helena once again asked her parents' permission to enter a convent. And again, they refused. Discouraged, the slender and lovely Helena decided to give up her dream. For almost a year, she worked as a maid for three women. By 1923 she decided that since she was not allowed to enter religious life, she would need a better-paying job that would enable her to buy fashionable clothes and attend dances with her sisters. Ignoring God's gentle, loving promptings in her soul to enter religious life, Helena obtained a job as maid and babysitter for the Sadowska family in Lodz.

One night at a dance, despite the lively music and the loud mix of voices, Helena suddenly saw Jesus. Stripped of his clothes, he stood next to her, his flesh covered with wounds. Though his eyes spoke to her of love, they also revealed his agonizing pain. When he then asked her why she kept delaying her entrance into a convent, the tone of his voice and the look on his divine face told her how much her delay grieved him. Not knowing how to reply, Helena left the dance by herself and headed to a nearby cathedral, where she begged God to tell her exactly what to do. Jesus advised her to go to Warsaw and enter a convent.

Helena returned home, told her sister what had happened, and asked her to relate her decision to their parents, Stanislaus and Marianna. Although knowing how much her parents would grieve over losing her tore at Helena's heart, she could wait no longer for their permission to enter religious life. She would have to trust Jesus, her merciful Lord and Master, to comfort and console her beloved parents. God wanted her to act—now.

With nothing except the dress she wore and a small bag of essentials, eighteen-year-old Helena set off for Warsaw to find a convent that would accept her. Upon her arrival in that city, not knowing anyone, she asked Mary, the mother of God, what she should do. Mary told her to go to a nearby village, where she would find a safe place to spend the night. Helena did so, and the next morning she traveled back to Warsaw, found a Catholic church, and entered. During Mass she asked God what she should do next. He told her to talk to the priest. After Mass she explained her situation to the priest, and he told her to go to the Warsaw home of a woman named Mrs. Aldona Lipszyc, who needed a housemaid. The woman hired her, and during her free time, Helena searched for a convent. She trusted that in his great love and mercy, Jesus would help her find the convent he had intended for her.

Pause: Recall a time in your life when God, in his merciful love for you, seemed to be leading you in a specific direction. How did you respond?

Faustina's Words

This evening, when I heard the hymn, "Good night, Holy Head of my Jesus," on the radio, my spirit was suddenly swept away to God's mysterious bosom, and I knew in what the greatness of a soul consists and what matters to God: love, love, and once again, love. And I understood how all that exists is saturated with God, and such a love of God inundated my soul that I am at a loss to describe it. Happy the soul that knows how to love unreservedly, for in this lies its greatness.[3]

Eternal Love, Depth of Mercy, O Triune Holiness, yet One God, whose bosom is full of love for all, as a good Father You scorn no one. O Love of God, Living Fountain, pour Yourself out upon us, Your unworthy creatures. May our misery not hold back the torrents of Your love, for indeed, there is no limit to Your mercy.[4]

Reflection

How can we become more aware of dwelling in God's merciful love? Since "God is love" (1 John 4:8), and God is infinite mercy, we can count on the fact that we already dwell in that merciful love, because he is everywhere present, within and around each of us. As the merciful, loving parent that he is, God loves each of us unconditionally. All we have to do is "Draw near to God, and he will draw near to you" (James 4:8). Each of us can "draw near" to God in countless ways and thus experience his unfathomable, merciful love enfolding us. Drawing near to God and getting to know him also help us to grow in our love for him.

Prayer is one of the foundational ways of getting to know, love, and experience God, but not just by our speaking to him. Getting to know God is like getting to know a fellow human being: we have to do a lot of listening to the other person in order to learn more about him or her. Faustina listened to God as he led her to religious life. Along each step of the way, through prayer, she relied on him to show her what to do.

Most of us will never experience the visions that Sr. Faustina had of Jesus, but we can learn to listen to God by mulling over a particular Scripture and allowing the Holy Spirit to help its truth sink deep into our souls. One of the fruits of the Holy Spirit is love (Galatians 5:22-23), and when we meditate on God's word in Scripture, we can count on the Holy Spirit to touch our hearts and convince our minds of his truth, which is love (1 John 4:8).

We can also get to know, love, and experience the God of love and mercy by keeping his commandments. As Faustina grew in her awareness of God's unconditional, merciful love for her, her desire to love and please him increased. When she realized that he still desired her to enter religious life, she persevered until she was accepted into a convent.

Do you sometimes think of God as a harsh judge, waiting to punish you? That type of negative thinking can cause you to fear him. It can also prevent you from growing in your awareness of his unconditional, merciful love for you.

Find a quiet spot where you can be alone with God. Sit or lie down, whichever is practical in your situation, and close your eyes. Take a few deep breaths, and then ask the Holy Spirit to help you recall recent times when God acted on your behalf to make difficult situations work out for your good, as well as for the good of those you love. You could repeat this spiritual exercise each evening before you sleep and thereby grow daily in your awareness of God's abiding, merciful love.

On New Year's Day 1937, Sr. Faustina made a resolution: "to see the image of God in every sister; all love of neighbor must flow from this motive."[5] Tomorrow during all your waking hours, practice visualizing God in each individual you encounter. Before going to sleep, examine your conscience to see if this practice helped you see Jesus in every person with whom you came in contact. Did your love for them, as well as for God, increase as a result?

❧ Read the "God's Word" section on p. 34 and meditate on the phrase "God is love." Since God is omnipresent and since he is love itself, visualize yourself nestled against his loving heart. Do this in times of stress, anxiety, depression, fatigue, or in any difficult situation. Allow yourself to totally relax in God's loving embrace, and let him fill you with his calming presence, which is merciful love.

❧ God asks us to love our neighbor as ourselves (Mark 12:31). This implies that we must love ourselves first. Do you truly love yourself as God desires? Do you take care of your body, soul, and mind to the best of your ability? When the responsibilities of daily life become too demanding, it might be tempting to deprive yourself of adequate rest, nutrition, exercise, and even prayer. What if each day, in addition to giving your body adequate rest, exercise, and nutrition, you also rest, exercise, and feed your soul? To give "rest" to your soul, you could spiritually place yourself in the tender heart of the Lord, as Sr. Faustina recommended. To "exercise" your soul, you could pray a silent "Jesus, I love you" or a Hail Mary every hour. And to "feed" your soul, you could read and meditate on Scripture.

❧ Jesus calls us to have mercy on and love even our enemies (Matthew 5:44). Do you have any "enemies" to whom you hesitate to show love and mercy because they've treated you unfairly or unkindly? If so, remember that mercy is a gift. It is not something anyone deserves. If God shows us merciful love, which we've certainly done nothing to deserve, doesn't he expect us to treat even our enemies in the same way? When it seems almost impossible to love and show mercy to your "enemies," ask Jesus to give you *his* merciful love for them and to love them *through* you. He will do it!

God's Word

Beloved, let us love one another, because love is from God; everyone who loves is born of God and knows God. Whoever does not love does not know God, for God is love. (1 John 4:7-8)

Closing Prayer: Dear Lord, fill me with your everlasting merciful love. Fill me to overflowing, so that your love and mercy spill out to everyone in my life. Always help me to love you with all the force of my soul and to know in my heart that you love me even more in return.

1. *Diary of Maria Faustina Kowalska: Divine Mercy in My Soul* (Stockbridge, MA: Marians of the Immaculate Conception, 1987), 1074.
2. *Diary*, 7.
3. *Diary*, 997.
4. *Diary*, 1307.
5. *Diary*, 861.

Meditation Two

As You Did It to Me: The Corporal Works of Mercy

Theme: Sr. Faustina believed Jesus when he said, "Truly I tell you, just as you did it to one of the least of these who are members of my family, you did it to me" (Matthew 25:40). In her devotion to the divine Redeemer whom she acknowledged in each individual, Faustina reached out to help anyone who needed her, especially through the corporal works of mercy.

Opening Prayer: Lord, you know my heart and how I want to serve you by helping all who need me, but you also know I can do nothing without you. So at all times, let your own unfathomable mercy flow through my body, mind, and soul to enable me to serve others as you desire.

About Faustina

Sr. Faustina's service to others began in early childhood and continued throughout her life. Whenever she recognized the needs of others, her heart burned with the desire to help them. In meeting their needs, she demonstrated her great love for her master, who said that when we do anything for anyone, we do it for him (see Matthew 25:40).

One day in 1937, Sr. Faustina's assigned duty was to respond to anyone who approached the convent's gated entrance. According to her diary, after struggling through the cold, rainy weather, a poor young man arrived at the gate. The sight of his tattered clothing and emaciated body seared Faustina's heart. The icy wind that had blown in through the door when she first opened it and the sight of the young man's bare feet and head told her that he must be nearly frozen. He asked her for something hot to eat. Even though she had never seen him before, she welcomed him inside to sit at the table. Then she hurried to the kitchen to prepare him a bowl of hot soup, into which she crumbled some bread for extra nourishment. When she placed the bowl in front of the young man, he eagerly consumed its contents, as if he had not eaten in days. "As I was taking the bowl from him," Faustina later wrote, "he gave me to know that He was the Lord of heaven and earth. When I saw Him as He was, He vanished from my sight."[1]

After returning to her assigned post inside the main entrance and while reflecting on what had just happened, Faustina heard the Lord speak in her soul. He praised her for her compassion for every poor person who came to the gate when she was on duty. And Jesus told her that because he wanted to experience her compassion himself, he had visited her in the form of the young beggar. This experience intensified Faustina's love for needy people, and she realized that wherever we are and at any time, we can find opportunities to actively serve and assist others.

Pause: In what ways do you serve and assist God's people through deeds of mercy?

Faustina's Words

I understand that mercy is manifold; one can do good always and everywhere and at all times. An ardent love of God sees all around itself constant opportunities to share itself through deed, word and prayer.[2]

O my Jesus, I know that a person's greatness is evidenced by his deeds and not by his words or feelings. It is the works that have come from us that will speak about us. My Jesus, do not allow me to daydream, but give me the courage and strength to fulfill Your holy will.[3]

Reflection

The seven corporal works of mercy in Christian tradition are feeding the hungry, giving drink to the thirsty, clothing the naked, ransoming the captives, sheltering the homeless, visiting the sick and imprisoned, and burying the dead. Whenever we allow ourselves to identify with someone in distress of any kind and then try to help them, we are demonstrating mercy. In doing so, we reflect God's own mercy.

When Jesus assumed his human nature through the incarnation, he at the same time brought to his humanity his divine person. But even though he is true God and true man, he humbled himself and became the servant of all, and he now calls us to do the same (see Philippians 2:4-7). Jesus wants us to follow him in service to those in need, especially those people we encounter each day.

However, we often find it easier to help people who are kind, of sound mind, and physically clean, rather than those who are caustic, mentally disturbed, or just plain filthy. When Faustina visited her childhood home, neighbors often brought their children to her, insisting that she hold them in her arms and kiss them. "They regarded this as a great favor,"[4] Faustina later wrote in her diary. What she found most difficult, though, was that many of the children were filthy. One in particular had diseased eyes that oozed pus. Nevertheless, Faustina fought her natural repugnance, took the child in her arms, and "kissed it twice, right on the infection, asking God to heal it."[5] Though God may never ask us to perform such a distasteful service, no matter who the Lord places in our path to serve, we can always ask the Holy Spirit to help us. And we can count on him doing exactly that because "it is God who is at work in you, enabling you both to will and to work for his good pleasure" (Philippians 2:13).

Because Christ reached out to all those in misery and identified himself with the "least" of his people, we as the body of Christ are called to do the same. But what is our response when we see a person suffering some type of misery that he created himself, perhaps through sin, poor management, or laziness? What if we know that the person in need will never be able to return the favor to us? And what if the person is our "enemy," for whatever reason? Jesus said, "If you do good to those who do good to you, what credit is that to you? . . . But love your enemies, do good, and lend, expecting nothing in return. Your reward will be great, and you will be children of the Most High; for he is kind to the ungrateful and the wicked. Be merciful, just as your Father is merciful" (Luke 6:33, 35-36). Who in your community or even among your relatives are your "enemies" or perhaps seem "undeserving" of mercy? Consider how God might be calling you to exercise the corporal works of mercy on their behalf.

❧ Read Matthew 25:31-46, and imagine the questions Jesus might ask you at the last judgment.: "Did you feed the hungry and give drink to the thirsty? When people were imprisoned—even 'imprisoned' in a nursing home—did you visit them? When people lacked adequate clothing—perhaps during the cold winter months—did you help clothe them? When strangers came to you—perhaps even a prodigal son or daughter (Luke 15:20-24)—did you welcome them?" Examine your conscience every evening to see when you performed the corporal works of mercy. Rejoice and give thanks for your good deeds. For the times you failed to perform works of mercy when an opportunity presented itself, simply ask God's forgiveness and ask him to help you take advantage of the next opportunity.

❧ What volunteer groups in your area are active in serving the poor and needy? Discern if God is calling you to participate in their merciful deeds. Remember that God may not ask you to do what someone else you know is doing to help the needy. Taking your personality and life situation into account, discern how God might be calling you to serve others, and then make St. Paul's words your own: "I can do all things through him who strengthens me" (Philippians 4:13).

❧ Using the simplest of tools—pencil or pen, and paper—try writing as a form of meditation. Recall a recent time when someone or some group did a merciful deed for you or for a member of your family. How did Christ's own mercy touch your heart and soul through that person's or that group's generous actions? Allow the memory of the joy and gratitude you experienced because of their good works to echo in your heart and inspire you to show God's mercy to others.

God's Word

The point is this: the one who sows sparingly will also reap sparingly, and the one who sows bountifully will also reap bountifully. Each of you must give as you have made up your mind, not reluctantly or under compulsion, for God loves a cheerful giver. And God is able to provide you with every blessing in abundance, so that by always having enough of everything, you may share abundantly in every good work. As it is written,

"He scatters abroad, he gives to the poor;
his righteousness endures forever."

He who supplies seed to the sower and bread for food will supply and multiply your seed for sowing and increase the harvest of your righteousness. (2 Corinthians 9:6-10)

Closing Prayer: My Jesus, your mercy and generosity are infinitely greater than I can ever imagine. Expand my heart, and fill it with your own merciful and generous Spirit. Make my heart sensitive to all those in need, and use me to spend my life doing good to all.

1. *Diary of Saint Maria Faustina Kowalska: Divine Mercy in My Soul* (Stockbridge, MA: Marians of the Immaculate Conception, 1987), 1312.

2. *Diary*, 1313.

3. *Diary*, 663.
4. *Diary*, 401.
5. *Diary*, 401.

Meditation Three

Come, O Blessed: The Spiritual Works of Mercy

Theme: In her love for the incarnate Christ who identifies himself with every person (Matthew 25:40), Sr. Faustina found joy in reaching out to help whoever needed her. In addition to serving others through the corporal works of mercy, she also performed the spiritual works of mercy, such as praying for others and counseling them.

Opening Prayer: Jesus, arouse in me the desire to help those in need. Help me to lovingly admonish, instruct, counsel, comfort, and forgive them. Inspire me to always pray for souls in need and to patiently bear all wrongs done to me. By your grace, Lord, I will spend the rest of my life glorifying your mercy by practicing mercy in whatever ways you call me.

About Faustina

Although Sr. Faustina faithfully served others through the corporal works of mercy, the spiritual works of mercy occupied the majority of her thirty-three years. Those works have traditionally included admonishing the sinner, instructing the ignorant, counseling the doubtful, comforting the sorrowful, bearing wrongs patiently, forgiving all injuries, and praying for the living and the dead.

Countless times throughout her life, Sr. Faustina practiced these works of mercy, relying on the gifts and fruits of the Holy Spirit to do so. In February 1935, for example, during the long train ride from the convent to her parents' cottage to see her dying mother, Faustina sensed that one of the passengers was experiencing a difficult battle within her soul. After a long period of silently praying for the woman, Faustina still sensed her inner struggle. "Finally, the lady turned to me," Faustina later wrote in her diary, "and asked if she was obliged to fulfill a certain promise which she had made to God."[1] Months before the train ride, when the woman was ready to take the exams that would qualify her to become a teacher, she had promised God that if he helped her to pass the exams, she would enter a religious congregation and devote her whole life to him. Now, during this train ride, Faustina told the woman that she definitely *was* obliged to keep the promise and that if she did not keep it, it would haunt her for the rest of her life. Because of Faustina's willingness to follow the promptings of the Holy Spirit in praying for and then counseling the schoolteacher, the troubled woman told Faustina that she would immediately begin the process of finding and joining a religious order. After promising to continue to pray for the woman, Faustina felt in her soul "the assurance that God would be generous with His grace."[2]

During her years with the Sisters of Our Lady of Mercy, Faustina had unlimited opportunities to practice one spiritual work of mercy in particular: bearing wrongs patiently. One day in the early 1930s, her superior assigned Faustina the duty of cleaning an elderly nun's room. While the younger nun tried to do the best job she could, the older one followed her around the whole time, saying, "You've left a speck of dust here and a spot on the floor there."[3] Whenever the elderly woman criticized Faustina's work, the young nun redid it at least a dozen times in an attempt to please her.

As if causing Sr. Faustina such grief were not enough, the elderly nun marched down the hall to complain to the mother superior, saying, "Mother, who is this careless sister who doesn't know how to work quickly?"[4] When the elderly nun returned to her room to continue her grumbling, Faustina did not try to defend herself; she merely continued cleaning. Later, in her diary, she told Jesus that the hard physical work did not tire her; what exhausted her were all the caustic words the nun had said to her while she cleaned.

Pause: Over the past week, when did you have an opportunity to bear a wrong patiently? How did you respond?

Faustina's Words

Help me, O Lord, that my heart may be merciful so that I myself may feel all the sufferings of my neighbor. I will refuse my heart to no one. I will be sincere even with those who, I know, will abuse my kindness. And I will lock myself up in the most merciful heart of Jesus.[5]

[*When Jesus asked Faustina to perform works of mercy, she replied,*] O my Jesus, You yourself must help me in everything, because You see how very little I am, and so I depend solely on Your goodness, O God.[6]

For there are three ways of performing an act of mercy: the merciful word, by forgiving and by comforting; secondly, if you can offer no word, then pray—that too is mercy; and thirdly, deeds of mercy. And when the Last Day comes, we shall be judged from this, and on this basis we shall receive the eternal verdict.[7]

Reflection

Sometimes it seems impossible to show compassion through an act of mercy to particular individuals in our lives. If we rely on our own strength and good will, it *is* impossible. But in baptism, we were joined to Christ and made "participants of the divine nature" (2 Peter 1:4). At the same time, we became temples of the Holy Spirit, and as Scripture says, "Do you not know that your body is a temple of the Holy Spirit within you, which you have from God, and that you are not your own? For you were bought with a price; therefore glorify God in your body" (1 Corinthians 6:19-20). The Holy Spirit waits eagerly within each of us to help us glorify God through works of mercy.

We are given specific gifts of the Holy Spirit to sustain us in practicing works of mercy and in showing compassion to all in need. These gifts—wisdom, understanding, counsel, fortitude, knowledge, piety, and fear of the Lord—help us to faithfully follow the promptings of the Holy Spirit when he inspires us to perform an act of mercy. As we allow him to work his loving will within us, he forms in us the fruits of the Spirit: "love, joy, peace, patience, kindness, generosity, faithfulness, gentleness, and self-control" (Galatians 5:22-23). And the more we perform works of mercy, the more these fruits can grow and develop in us.

Recall a time when you knew a particular person in your life was not following God's will. You may have wanted to steer that person in the right direction but at the same time did not want to hurt his feelings, lose his friendship, or sound self-righteous. What did you do? If you ignored the opportunity to lovingly suggest what you thought God was calling him to do, how did you feel? Maybe your lack of courage still haunts you. In the coming week, ask the Holy Spirit to make you aware of situations in which he wants you to practice a spiritual work of mercy. Then ask him to work through you to accomplish that act of mercy.

❧ Like Sr. Faustina, have you "learned that certain people have a special gift for vexing others"?[8] The next time someone "vexes" you, trust the Holy Spirit to help you in "bearing patiently" the individual's annoying behavior toward you.

❧ To faithfully and consistently carry out the spiritual works of mercy, we need the gifts of the Holy Spirit. If you ever think that because you do not "deserve" such gifts, God would never grant them to you, recall Jesus' words: "If you then, who are evil, know how to give good gifts to your children, how much more will the heavenly Father give the Holy Spirit to those who ask him!" (Luke 11:13). Spend time in prayer during the next week or two, asking the Holy Spirit to give you one of his gifts or fruits (see Isaiah 11:2; Galatians 5:22-23). Ask one of your friends or your spouse to pray with you to receive this gift and then to hold you accountable for exercising it.

❧ Even when you are ill or prevented by any other reason from reaching out to help people, you can always pray for them. Tonight before you go to sleep or tomorrow morning before you begin your day's work, think of three people you know who need your prayers. Write their names on a sheet of paper or in your journal. One at a time, lift each of them up to God and say the following short prayer: "In your mercy, Jesus, please heal him (or her) in all ways—physically, emotionally, and especially spiritually." Next, think of three people who have died. Write down their names as well. Then ask the Lord, "Take their souls to heaven and comfort those left behind to mourn."

❧ Do you know someone who is sorrowing? You can comfort them by visiting them or by calling them on the telephone and simply listening as they express their grief.

❧ If you are a teacher, coach, or parent, every day is filled with opportunities to "instruct the ignorant." But no matter what your job, age, financial status, or health, you can at all times "instruct the ignorant" by the example you set for others in everything you do. As you go about your day, consider who might be noticing your behavior, taking "instruction" from it, and then following your example. Each morning during your prayer time, ask the Lord to help you grow in awareness of the example you set.

God's Word

For we are what he has made us, created in Christ Jesus for good works, which God prepared beforehand to be our way of life. (Ephesians 2:10)

Teach me to do your will,
for you are my God.
Let your good spirit lead me
on a level path. (Psalm 143:10)

Closing Prayer: Heavenly Father, may you be praised forever for reaching down to sinful humanity and showing us your mercy. Though I am a weak, small, sinful creature, show your mercy through me by using my every breath, heartbeat, thought, and moment to practice those "good works" you have "prepared beforehand" for me to do (see Ephesians 2:10). I will bless you forever for using me to serve others.

1. *Diary of Saint Maria Faustina Kowalska: Divine Mercy in My Soul* (Stockbridge, MA: Marians of the Immaculate Conception, 1987), 396.
2. *Diary*, 396.
3. *Diary*, 181.
4. *Diary*, 181.
5. *Diary*, 163.
6. *Diary*, 742.
7. *Diary*, 1158.
8. *Diary*, 182.

Meditation Four

Mother of Mercy, Your Mother

Theme: Not only did she show her devotion to Christ and his mother through praying the Rosary, but Faustina also strove to imitate the virtues of the mother of God. Subsequently, Jesus gave these virtues to Faustina through Mary, who inspired and helped the young nun to practice them, because as Faustina knew, the more she loved and imitated the mother of God, the better she came to know and love God himself.

Opening Prayer: Dear Jesus, in your incomparable love, you chose to come to us through your immaculate mother. Through her, the virginal and sacred vessel, grant me the virtues and graces I need to love and serve you with all my heart. Help me to love and honor her as you do.

About Faustina

Throughout her life, Faustina experienced many visions of the mother of God. On August 5, 1935, on the feast of Our Lady of

Mercy, Sr. Faustina was struggling internally with a problem she could not seem to resolve. Seeking God's answer, she attended that day's first Mass. Still without a solution to her problem, she attended the second Mass. When Faustina silently asked Mary to help her discern God's answer to her problem, within seconds the mother of God appeared to her, poised on the church's altar and radiating her rare beauty.

Mary descended from the altar, gracefully glided toward Faustina's pew, and serenely stood before the young nun. Mary embraced her and said, "I am Mother to you all, thanks to the unfathomable mercy of God."[1] Mary continued speaking gently to Sr. Faustina, exhorting her to be courageous and not to fear anything or anyone that might threaten her. "But fix your gaze upon the Passion of My Son," said Mary, "and in this way you will be victorious."[2] We, too, can freely apply her words to our lives.

From the time Faustina could appreciate the virtue of purity, she asked Mary to obtain that virtue for her and to help her to practice it her entire life. The young nun wanted to belong solely to Jesus—body, mind, and soul. During a Mass in 1929, Sr. Faustina experienced the tangible closeness of God. Fearing that it was an illusion created by Satan to deceive her, she tried to ignore the strong presence. But before Communion, Jesus suddenly appeared to Faustina, wearing a white garment secured at his waist by a length of golden material. The Lord told her, "I give you eternal love that your purity may be untarnished and as a sign that you will never be subject to temptations against purity."[3] As if it were a symbol of that "eternal love," Jesus removed the golden material from his waist and secured it around Faustina's.

According to Faustina's diary, after Christ's appearance that day, temptations against purity never attacked her for the rest of her life. What role did the mother of Jesus play in regard to this virtuous gift? Faustina wrote in her diary, "I later understood that this was one of the greatest graces which the Most Holy Virgin Mary had obtained for me, as for many years I had been asking this grace of Her."[4] The reception of such a remarkable grace inspired Faustina to practice an ever-increasing devotion to Mary.

Throughout Faustina's remaining years, Mary taught her, above all, how to show greater devotion to God. From Mary, Faustina learned how to love God within her soul and how to obey him at all times. "O Mary, You are joy, because through You God descended to earth [and] into my heart."[5] But the graces and virtues were not given to Faustina because she was already perfect. According to her diary, these graces were given to her because she was "the weakest of all people; this is why the Almighty has surrounded me with His special mercy."[6] God, through his mother, will also help us to live grace-filled, virtuous lives if we but ask for them.

Pause: Consider what graces and virtues you would like to practice throughout your life. Ask Mary to obtain them for you from her divine Son. Trust that the tiny seeds of virtue she will plant within you will—with the life-giving "waters" of time, prayer, grace, and practice—grow to feed, not only your soul, but the souls of others, too.

Faustina's Words

Mary is my Instructress, who is ever teaching me how to live for God. My spirit brightens up in Your gentleness and Your humility, O Mary.[7]

I look for no happiness beyond my own interior where God dwells. I rejoice that God dwells within me; here I abide with Him unendingly; it is here that my greatest intimacy with Him exists; here I dwell with Him in safety; here is a place not probed by the human eye. The Blessed Virgin encourages me to commune with God in this way.[8]

Reflection

As the first disciple of Christ, Mary set a powerful example for Faustina and inspired the young nun to imitate her. Faustina knew Mary would always lead her to Jesus. After all, since Mary had known her divine Son intimately, Faustina knew she could place absolute trust in her. Through Christ, Mary was Faustina's mother—and ours, too.

In what ways did Faustina want to become more like Mary? In her dealings with the wayward girls who lived in the homes supported and run by the Sisters of Our Lady of Mercy, Faustina wanted to imitate the tenderness Mary had shown as she cradled her newborn son. In bearing courageously her sufferings of body, mind, and soul, Faustina wanted to imitate the strength Mary had exhibited as she stood beneath the cross of her crucified son. As Mary had faithfully and uncomplainingly carried out her daily duties, so, too, did Faustina want to carry out her own duties. And Faustina wanted to imitate Mary's spirit of contemplation as she "treasured all these things in her heart" (Luke 2:51).

The spirituality of Faustina calls us to offer our entire beings to Jesus, just as his mother has done, and to depend on her to help us serve him all the days of our lives, in whatever ways he desires.

During Mass on the feast of the Immaculate Conception in 1937, Sr. Faustina saw the incredibly beautiful mother of Jesus. Mary smiled as she spoke to Faustina, telling the young nun that God had commanded her to be Faustina's mother in a special way and that she, in turn, wanted Faustina to be her special child. Mary's desire applies to us, too, because in Jesus' agony on the cross, he made his mother the mother of us all (John 19:26-27). With confidence, make an act of consecration to

Mary. Say to her, "Be my mother in a special way, dear Mary, and let me know that I, like Faustina, am your special child."

At another Mass on the feast of the Immaculate Conception, this time in 1936, an exquisitely lovely Mary appeared to Sr. Faustina. As Mary spoke to her, a brilliant light radiated from Mary's entire person, and she said she was "Queen of heaven and earth."[9] At that moment, she embraced Faustina and told her that as the mother of Jesus, she always felt compassion for her. Have you experienced the compassion of Mary? If not, go to her with your needs. Ask her to have compassion on you and to intercede for you before the throne of her son.

❧ Consider again Mary's advice to Faustina: "Be courageous. Do not fear apparent obstacles, but fix your gaze upon the Passion of My Son, and in this way you will be victorious."[10] To discover how meditating on Christ's passion makes us courageous, spend some quiet moments gazing at a crucifix. The size of the crucifix makes no difference, as long as Christ crucified is depicted on it. Meditate on his agony as he hung there. Consider Jesus' unconditional love for you that led him to his passion and death on the cross in order to redeem you. Reflect on the following Scripture passage, which will help you in your meditation to find courage and strength in Christ's love for you: "For while we were still weak, at the right time Christ died for the ungodly. Indeed, rarely will anyone die for a righteous person—though perhaps for a good person someone might actually dare to die.

But God proves his love for us in that while we still were sinners Christ died for us" (Romans 5:6-8).

❧ Throughout her years as a religious sister, amid her ongoing physical and emotional suffering, Sr. Faustina received many graces, virtues, and insights from God. Mary told Faustina that these graces were not intended just for her own good, but for the good of every soul, whether on earth or in purgatory. What graces, virtues, or spiritual insights has God given you? For example, this past Sunday during the priest's homily, did something he say speak to your heart? Have you recently received encouragement and inner strength to face and overcome an obstacle that up until that time had threatened to overwhelm and defeat you or someone you love? Whatever God has given you, try to find ways in the coming week to share it in some way with others who may be experiencing difficulties of some sort.

❧ We can pray informally to Mary at any time for any reason, but we can also choose to use formal prayers. One prayer in particular, which has retained its popularity since its inception during medieval times, is the Rosary. Through our thoughtfully reciting the Rosary's Our Fathers and Hail Marys, our imaginations can place us on the scene with Jesus and Mary as we journey with them through the gospel stories. If you cannot find enough time to pray the entire Rosary, pray one Hail Mary whenever you can.

God's Word

Meanwhile, standing near the cross of Jesus were his mother, and his mother's sister, Mary the wife of Clopas, and Mary Magdalene. When Jesus saw his mother and the disciple whom he loved standing beside her, he said to his mother, "Woman, here is your son." Then he said to the disciple, "Here is your mother." And from that hour the disciple took her into his own home. (John 19:25-27)

Closing Prayer: Hail Mary, full of grace, the Lord is with thee. Blessed art thou among women, and blessed is the fruit of thy womb, Jesus. Holy Mary, mother of God, pray for us sinners, now and at the hour of our death. Amen.

1. *Diary of Saint Maria Faustina Kowalska: Divine Mercy in My Soul* (Stockbridge, MA: Marians of the Immaculate Conception, 1987), 449.
2. *Diary*, 449.
3. *Diary*, 40.
4. *Diary*, 40.
5. *Diary*, 40.
6. *Diary*, 1099.
7. *Diary*, 620.
8. *Diary*, 454.
9. *Diary*, 805.
10. *Diary*, 449.

Meditation Five

God's Will, Your Daily Food

Theme: At all times and in all situations, Sr. Faustina sought to do the will of God. She called his will her "daily food."[1] She also readily admitted that without God's grace, she would never be able to obey him.

Opening Prayer: Jesus, you who faithfully did the will of the Father in all things, grant me the grace to always and everywhere do his will, even when doing so might bring hardship and suffering into my life. Like you, help me to not count the cost of obeying, but rather to gladly accept the Father's will, knowing it comes from a heart overflowing with love for me. Make your own words echo forever in my soul: "Your will be done" (Matthew 6:10).

About Faustina

Throughout her life, Faustina always did her best to discern and do God's will. One circumstance in her life, in particular, demonstrates this virtue. On the evening of June 9, 1935, while

Sr. Faustina was strolling in the convent garden, she received her first message from Jesus about his desire for her to establish a new congregation of sisters, apart from the Congregation of the Sisters of Our Lady of Mercy to which she belonged. The purpose of the new congregation would be to continuously beg God to have mercy on sinful humanity and to spread devotion to his divine mercy.[2] But like Moses, who told God he lacked the skills and influence to carry out the tasks the Lord set before him (Exodus 3:11; 4:1, 10), Faustina felt totally inadequate to take on this new responsibility. Like Moses, she reminded God of her many weaknesses. But just as the Lord had told Moses, Jesus assured Faustina, "Do not fear; I myself will make up for everything that is lacking in you."[3] Still unconvinced, she continued to give Jesus excuses.

Twenty days later, on June 29, Faustina spoke with her spiritual director, Msgr. Michael Sopocko,[4] and told him what Jesus was asking of her. The young nun expected Msgr. Sopocko to tell her that the Lord could not possibly want to use someone like her to establish a new religious order of sisters. After all, Faustina had received only three winters of schooling, and she had no money, influence, or significant skills. But to her surprise, the priest assured her that God likes to use the weak to carry out his plans.

Later that month,[5] Jesus told Faustina she would have to overcome many obstacles to establish the new congregation. However, during Communion at Mass the next day, God gave

Faustina such inner strength and courage about the prospect of establishing the new community that she exulted in his goodness. In spite of her many weaknesses and the many hardships she knew were ahead of her, she now felt "ready for every beck and call"[6] of his will. She knew that the words Jesus spoke to St. Paul also applied to her: "My grace is sufficient for you, for power is made perfect in weakness" (2 Corinthians 12:9). And along with Paul, Faustina agreed that "I am content with weaknesses, insults, hardships, persecutions, and calamities for the sake of Christ; for whenever I am weak, then I am strong" (2 Corinthians 12:10).

From June 1935 until her death on October 5, 1938, Faustina's efforts to establish the new community met with endless obstacles, just as Jesus had warned her. Although Jesus continued to encourage her, at the same time her superiors and many of the priests she consulted discouraged her. Some said that God could not possibly want someone like her to establish a congregation, or they would simply put her off by telling her to wait. However, Jesus commanded Faustina to always obey the will of her superiors and spiritual directors in regard to establishing the new community, even if their will conflicted with his. On April 1, 1938, for example, when Faustina asked Jesus how she could possibly do his will, he replied, "It is not for you to know how this will come about. Your duty is to be faithful to My grace and to do always what is within your power and what obedience allows you to do."[7] By "obedience," he meant obedience to those in authority over her.

Finally, after much suffering, Faustina was able to be at peace with the situation. She would not see the establishment of a new congregation in her lifetime, but she had done everything in her power to obey her Lord and her superiors.

Pause: Reflect on Faustina's determination to obey God by obeying those in authority over her. Through what "authorities" might you discern God's will for your life?

Faustina's Words

There is one word I heed and continually ponder; it alone is everything to me; I live by it and die by it, and it is the holy will of God. It is my daily food. My whole soul listens intently to God's wishes. I do always what God asks of me, although my nature often quakes and I feel that the magnitude of these things is beyond my strength. I know well what I am of myself, but I also know what the grace of God is, which supports me.[9]

Reflection

To us, it may seem that it was easy for the saints to obey God's will. But we see from Faustina's example that even saints struggle in discerning and obeying God's will. Like many of the saints, Faustina received gifts from the Lord such as bilocation (the ability to be in more than one place at one time); prophecy; reading of souls; and visions of Jesus, Mary, and her guardian angel. But even those gifts did not make obeying God less of a struggle for her. In one of her 1937 diary entries, she explained, "These gifts are merely ornaments of the soul, but constitute neither its essence nor its perfection. My sanctity and perfection consist in the close union of my will with the will of God."[10]

Each day we have to make countless decisions. Confusion can cloud our minds as we struggle over questions such as, "What should I do about this?" or "What will people think if I do that?" or "What will happen if I fail?" When we finally manage to lift our thoughts above the turmoil, we ask God what *he* wants us to do. Faustina did not always trust the directions God seemed to be sending her because she knew that Satan often "disguises himself as an angel of light" (2 Corinthians 11:14). On Holy Thursday 1936, for example, while trying to discern God's will for her, Sr. Faustina sensed that Satan was mocking her, warning her about all that she would have to suffer if she obeyed God. After what seemed like hours of agonizing over whether it was truly the voice of God or merely the voice of the powers of darkness, Faustina attended Mass. At the very moment she received holy Communion, she silently asked God, "Let whatever You have decided upon happen to me."[11] Moments later Jesus spoke to her soul, telling her to seek confirmation of his will through those he had placed in authority over her. "And do only that for which you obtain permission," Jesus continued. "Do not be upset, and fear nothing; I am with you."[12]

Like Faustina, we, too, sometimes doubt our own discernment of God's will; but we, too, can seek confirmation of his will from those in authority over us, whether that be a priest, spouse, parent, religious sister or brother, counselor, teacher, or trusted friend. Like Faustina, we can listen for God's voice speaking to us through them, as well as through Scripture and the Church. Once we discern God's will, we can then ask Jesus to enable us to accept it, as well as to carry it out, even when doing so might bring us hardship and suffering. And we can trust and be assured that no matter what God asks us to do, his will calls to us from a heart overflowing with love.

❧ As members of the body of Christ, we are called to obey Church teachings. Have you ever struggled with something the Church teaches, wondering if obeying the Church in that matter was truly obeying God? If so, seek direction from trustworthy people who may be able to guide you to a better understanding of that teaching. Be open to allowing God to touch your heart and soul through their words.

❧ From your experiences in discerning God's will, you have probably learned to listen carefully for his gentle advice and his quiet guidance (see 1 Kings 19:12), whether it comes through a confidant, Scripture, your conscience, the Church, or even your own reasoning. Is there a recent decision you have discerned but still have doubts about? One way to test what you *think* God is telling you to do is by asking the Holy Spirit to give you peace about it only if it truly is God's will. When that peace comes, rest in it, express gratitude for God's loving will, and confidently—even joyfully—obey.

❧ In today's culture, "doing your own thing" is promoted as a virtue. Reflect on these two Scripture verses: "We must obey God rather than any human authority" (Acts 5:29) and "For my thoughts are not your thoughts, nor are your ways my ways, says the LORD" (Isaiah 55:8). Recall a recent occasion when you decided to obey God rather than listen to what the world would have you do. Did you feel stupid and foolish for your obedience to God? The next time you feel foolish for obeying God, call to mind the fact that "God's foolishness is wiser than human wisdom, and God's weakness is stronger than human strength" (1 Corinthians 1:25).

❧ Reflect on the "Opening Prayer" of this meditation. What decision are you struggling with today? Are you willing to submit your will to your heavenly Father's? If you are still struggling, simply ask the Holy Spirit to help you declare in your heart, always and everywhere, "Your will be done."

❧ In order to surrender to God's will—even when his will seems totally against what you believe to be "good" for you or those you love—find a quiet, comfortable spot, close your eyes, and slowly repeat in your mind and heart, "God is love" (1 John 4:8). As you do so, relax and yield your will to Love, who dwells within you and who desires only the best for you.

God's Word

Jesus said to them, "My food is to do the will of him who sent me and to complete his work." (John 4:34)

So do not be foolish, but understand what the will of the Lord is. (Ephesians 5:17)

Closing Prayer:

Teach me to do your will,
  for you are my God.
Let your good spirit lead me
  on a level path. (Psalm 143:10)

1. *Diary of Saint Maria Faustina Kowalska: Divine Mercy in My Soul* (Stockbridge, MA: Marians of the Immaculate Conception, 1987), 652.

2. *Diary*, 435.

3. *Diary*, 435.

4. *Diary*, 436.

5. *Diary*, 439.
6. *Diary*, 439.
7. *Diary*, 1650.
8. *Diary*, n. 96.
9. *Diary*, 652.
10. *Diary*, 1107.
11. *Diary*, 644.
12. *Diary*, 645.

Meditation Six

Friendship with Jesus

Theme: From the beginning, God created us to share in his eternal friendship. In spite of any sins and weaknesses on our part, he still invites us to draw ever closer to him, to intimately commune with him, and to allow him to transform us into his holy people who are filled to overflowing with his love. Jesus called Faustina the "apple"[1] of his eye, someone he valued and cherished. He invited her to accept his divine friendship, which he promised would never end. He said he wanted all of us to "snuggle close"[2] to his merciful heart, where we will find peace and joy.

Opening Prayer: Dear God, how can you love me so much that you would want to shelter me in your eternal friendship? You even call me the "apple" of your eye (Deuteronomy 32:10)! You know my sins and weaknesses, and yet you call me to yourself, to your divine friendship. Here I am, Jesus; take me and never let me go.

About Faustina

Although from childhood Faustina had pledged her entire life to Jesus and had accepted his divine friendship, she sought to solidify in a formal way her personal commitment to him. On May 1, 1933, after almost eight years of preparation since first entering the Congregation of the Sisters of Our Lady of Mercy as a postulant, Sr. Faustina achieved that goal. From the moment she awoke that beautiful spring morning, she was consumed with the thought that today she would publicly pledge herself to her Lord, her spouse, her best friend. She would make a full commitment to the congregation, making her vows of poverty, chastity, and obedience.

During that day's Mass for perpetual vows, Faustina offered herself to God. "Today I place my heart on the paten where Your Heart has been placed, O Jesus,"[3] she silently prayed. She privately pledged undying faithfulness and love to Jesus, her best friend. Then, on the chapel floor before the altar, she prostrated herself beneath the pall, a large black cloth symbolizing death to the world. With the other sisters professing final vows and with those in the pews, she recited Psalm 129, the same one that was recited at funerals. While under the pall, Faustina begged Jesus to prevent her from ever again offending him "by even the smallest sin or imperfection."[4] She desired that nothing mar their eternal friendship. As the bells always did for Polish funerals, that day they tolled out their declaration that Sr. Faustina was now dead to the world but alive in Christ. Out of her overflowing love for God, she promised to live the rest of her life for him and him alone. Today he would become her "most beloved Spouse."[5]

On that day, Jesus accepted her silent as well as vocalized vows, and he spoke to her soul, assuring her that their hearts would remain united for all eternity. While still beneath the pall, Faustina not only prayed for herself but for the whole world. Addressing God as her "dearest Bridegroom," she thanked him for that day and told him, "But above all, O my Jesus, I thank You for Your Heart—it is all I need."[6]

When Bishop Stanislaus Rospond sprinkled holy water over Faustina and the others who had lain beneath the pall, he said to them, "Rise, you who are dead to the world, and Jesus Christ will give you light."[7] As the bishop placed the ring on Faustina's finger, symbolizing her betrothal to Christ, she felt God's presence spread through her entire being. From that day forward, her relationship with Jesus grew in intimacy, and like a true spouse, she knew she would never want to live without him, her best friend.

Pause: How is your own relationship with God similar to a relationship between friends? How is it different?

Faustina's Words

Jesus, Friend of a lonely heart, You are my haven, You are my peace. You are my salvation, You are my serenity in moments of struggle and amidst an ocean of doubts. You are the bright ray that lights up the path of my life.[8]

O Lord, I am inundated with Your grace. I sense that a new life has entered into me and, above all, I feel Your love in my heart. That is enough for me. O Lord, I will glorify the omnipotence of Your mercy for all eternity. Encouraged by Your goodness, I will confide to You all the sorrows of my heart.

[Jesus responded:] "Tell me all, My child, hide nothing from Me, because My loving Heart, the Heart of your Best Friend, is listening to you."[9]

Your friendship is more tender and subtle than the scent of a rose, and yet it is stronger than death.[10]

Reflection

We may never join a religious order as did Sr. Faustina, but her experiences can inspire us and lead us into a more intimate friendship with God, who created us to share in his own eternal life. When our first parents sinned, they broke their ties of friendship with God. Sin darkens our lives, too, but God offers us hope and light. He calls us to accept his forgiveness through the atoning sacrifice of Christ, restoring us to holiness and to his precious friendship.[11] We can have confidence that he will do this because "nothing will be impossible with God" (Luke 1:37).

At some point during 1933, Sr. Faustina wrote about the spiritual counsel given to her by the Jesuit priest Fr. Joseph

Andrasz. To our own lives, we can apply his advice on how to act in the presence of others. Fr. Andrasz told her to always treat others like true friends because Jesus had first given his love and friendship to her. She must behave in a manner that would bring joy and happiness to those around her, even if she only touched their lives for a moment. No matter how poorly—even cruelly—some people treated her during her convent years, Faustina tried to follow Fr. Andrasz's advice and treat everyone with respect, dignity, and compassion, even the poor beggars who approached the convent gate.

We, too, are called to live our lives in intimate friendship with God, just as Faustina did. In this friendship, God expects us to share with him our joys and sorrows, just as we would with an earthly friend. Because he dwells in our souls, we can at all times and in all places communicate spiritually with him. He waits for us to embrace him with our hearts and minds so that he can envelop us in his love.

We can develop an intimacy with God—and at the same time grow in holiness—by spending time with him in reading Scripture, in public as well as in private worship, in meditation, and by simply "listening" to him through contemplation. By doing all these things, we will get to know him *personally* rather than merely knowing *about* him. The better we know God, the more we will become like him in holiness and love. If we live holy lives within the embrace of his intimate friendship, we will also die in his grace and friendship and live forever (see 1 John 2:17).

From our friendship with God, we can go forth to extend love and friendship to all his people. Friendship is a gift from God, to be used to draw ourselves and our friends closer to him. If a particular friendship does not help us to grow closer to the Lord or to grow in holiness, we might want to question its validity. We all hunger for true friendships with special souls who will help us to see ourselves as the valuable and beloved children of God that we are. In the end, it is our intimacy with Jesus that affects how strong and deep our friendships with his people grow.

Jesus called Faustina "the apple of his eye." Keeping in mind that the term refers to something or someone who is cherished, ponder how *you* could be the apple of God's eye, his beloved friend. Your sins and weaknesses tell you that the Lord would never put you in that category. But consider the fact that when he chose his disciples, Jesus did not necessarily choose scholars, politicians, or temple leaders. He did not even look for "perfect" people who had never sinned. After all, he was creating a family, a family not so different from your own. Consider who he chose: fishermen, craftsmen, and other very common people. Their past did not matter to Jesus, and neither does yours. Allow yourself to accept his love and divine friendship. Hear him say to you, "You are the apple of my eye" (see Deuteronomy 32:10).

Think of your closest friends. What are their virtues and other attributes? How have your relationships with them helped you to grow in the same qualities? Friends who lead us to greater holiness reflect God's own friendship with us and what he is trying to do in our lives. Write a note to one of your special friends, thanking him or her for helping you grow closer to God. Promise yourself that you will continue to grow in holiness by imitating your friend's virtues.

❧ Have you ever felt isolated and friendless? Consider visiting, calling, or writing someone you know who might be feeling that way right now. By showing concern, love, and friendship to the sick, the elderly, the homebound, or anyone suffering in any way, you will help them to see—in you—Jesus, who longs to be their best friend. And in reaching out to them, you will forget about your own loneliness because you will realize that your "best friend" is always there for you. Like Faustina, you can truly say, "I am never alone, because He is my constant companion."[12]

❧ Jesus said the two greatest commandments are to love God with all your heart, soul, mind, and strength and to love your neighbor as yourself (see Mark 12:28-31). With that Scripture passage in mind, do you think it is possible to love others and to be a true friend to them if you do not first love and befriend yourself? In what ways do you love yourself as a true friend would? What are some of the ways in which you treat yourself with disrespect, disgust, impatience, or anything other than kindness? Make a list of what you like about yourself. Add to this list the qualities in yourself for which others have complimented or even praised you. Then thank God for those qualities, and ask him to help you accept yourself as he made you.

Even though our enemies can hurt us, our friends, who know so much more about us, can hurt us even more. When has a friend hurt you in some way? Pray for that person, and ask God to help you forgive him or her and then to let go of the pain.

God's Word

You are my friends if you do what I command you. (John 15:14)

The friendship of the Lord is for
those who fear him,
and he makes his covenant
known to them. (Psalm 25:14)

Some friends play at friendship
but a true friend sticks closer
than one's nearest kin. (Proverbs 18:24)

Faithful friends are a sturdy shelter:
whoever finds one has found a treasure. (Sirach 6:14)

Closing Prayer: Jesus, you are my treasure, my dearest friend. Whenever I feel lonely and isolated, remind me that you never leave me, not even for a second. Thank you, Lord, for your love and faithfulness. Use me to bring your true friendship to all those in my life.

1. *Diary of Saint Maria Faustina Kowalska: Divine Mercy in My Soul* (Stockbridge, MA: Marians of the Immaculate Conception, 1987), 1489.
2. *Diary*, 1074.
3. *Diary*, 239.
4. *Diary*, 239.
5. *Diary*, 240.
6. *Diary*, 240.
7. Sophia Michalenko, *Mercy My Mission* (Stockbridge, MA: Congregation of Marians, 1987), 48.
8. *Diary*, 247.
9. *Diary*, 1486.
10. *Diary*, 1575.
11. United States Catholic Conference, *Catechism of the Catholic Church, Second Edition* (Libreria Editrice Vaticana: United States Catholic Conference, Inc., 1997), 1468.
12. *Diary*, 318.

MEDITATION SEVEN

The Most Holy Trinity

Theme: Through faith, Sister Faustina experienced God's drawing her into his "inner life,"[1] where she was immersed in love and grew to know the Father, Son, and Holy Spirit as one majestic unity, the holy Trinity. In the depths of this one true God, she found mercy, joy, and peace.

Opening Prayer: Blessed Trinity, all praise, glory, and honor to you! Though you did not need any creature to make you happy, in your great love and mercy you created us so that we could share in your eternal triune life. One God in three persons, in your unfathomable goodness you have called me, a sinner, to love you. You, who are everything, drown my sins and misery in your infinite goodness and love. By your grace, eternal holy Trinity, may I love and serve you with my entire being, both now and forever.

ABOUT FAUSTINA

Sr. Faustina wanted to better understand the Trinity because she knew that the more we know God, the more we love him. She was well aware of her own shortcomings and lack of theological training; after all, she had only three short years of formal schooling. Nevertheless, one day in the convent chapel in 1928, she asked God to reveal himself to her in the fullness of his triune being, so that she could love him as he deserved and desired.

At that moment, unaware of anyone or anything else in the chapel, Faustina opened her mind, heart, and soul to whatever God wished to reveal to her. "I absolutely wanted to know and fathom who God is,"[2] she later wrote. Just like the description in Scripture of being "caught up into Paradise" (2 Corinthians 12:4), in the convent chapel that day, Faustina's spirit was "caught up into what seemed to be the next world."[3] In that "world," she saw an intense light that she could not approach. Within that great light, she could perceive three separate light sources, the meaning of which she could not grasp. Then, even more mysterious, undecipherable words rose from the light sources. Faustina watched in awe as the words, which appeared as lightning, "encircled heaven and earth."[4] Unable to comprehend the meaning of the words, she was sad. But then, in his merciful love, Christ appeared out of the intense light. Later Faustina described him as "our dearly beloved Savior, unutterably beautiful with His shining Wounds."[5]

Still unaware of anyone or anything else in the convent chapel, Faustina heard a voice speak from out of the intense light: "Who God is in His Essence, no one will fathom, neither the mind of Angels nor of man."[6]

Jesus then said to Faustina, "Get to know God by contemplating His attributes."[7] For the rest of her short life, the young nun did her best to learn about and meditate on God's attributes, those qualities that characterize the triune God, which include love, light, life, truth, wisdom, power, joy, peace, and mercy. The more Faustina contemplated the Creator, the more she realized how unfathomable he really is. She also realized that if she did know all there was to know about God, he would no longer be the infinite Creator but some finite creature like herself.[8] This truth allowed her to accept her own finite human nature and limitations, which she realized were shared by all people, even the most brilliant theologians, mystics, and saints.

This knowledge of herself did not discourage Faustina or deter her from further contemplating the holy Trinity. Neither did it stop God from further revealing himself, little by little, to her. One day in 1935, during Mass, God allowed Faustina to know more fully the oneness of the equality and majesty of the three divine persons: Father, Son, and Holy Spirit. Though her soul was drawn into "communion with these Three,"[9] she later was unable to describe what happened during that communion. But she did understand and later write that when we are united with one of the three persons in the Trinity, we are "united to the whole Blessed Trinity, for this Oneness is indivisible."[10]

On November 27, 1936, in spirit, Sr. Faustina once again experienced heaven. There she marveled at the beauty and happiness enjoyed by those who die in God's grace. She witnessed all the inhabitants of heaven praising and glorifying God, who shared his infinite happiness with them. In turn, those souls were able to contemplate the holy Trinity, even though they could never fully comprehend it. All of this brought great comfort and joy to Faustina's soul, and she rejoiced in her own finiteness, which served to magnify, by comparison, God's unfathomable infinity.

Pause: Reflect on the fact that you, like Faustina and all people of all time, will never be able to fully fathom the triune God, even when you reach heaven and see him face-to-face.

Faustina's Words

Interiorly I saw God looking at us with great pleasure. I remained alone with the Heavenly Father. At that moment, I had a deeper knowledge of the Three Divine Persons, whom we shall contemplate for all eternity and, after millions of years, shall discover that we have just barely begun our contemplation.[11]

The Holy Trinity grants me Its life abundantly, by the gift of the Holy Spirit. The Three Divine Persons live in me. When God loves, He loves with all His Being, with all the power of His Being. If God has loved me in this way, how should I respond—I, His spouse?[12]

Reflection

Even though we may never enjoy mystical experiences of the blessed Trinity as Faustina did, by faith we can believe in, accept, and embrace the fact that the triune God is and always will be a mystery to us. We do know that the Trinity is undivided, even though consisting of three persons. We know, too, that when we pray to Jesus, we are at the same time praying to God the Father and God the Holy Spirit. Theologians over the centuries have tried to help us better understand the Trinity through analogies. You may already have heard the analogy between an egg and the Trinity. Though the egg contains three separate parts—white, yolk, and shell—it remains one entity. So, too, the holy Trinity is three divine persons yet one creative, energizing reality. Because the blessed Trinity is a "communion of the Father and the Son in the Holy Spirit,"[13] we can make an analogy between it and the "communion" that the members of a Christian family form.

Though Scripture does not specifically mention the Trinity, God's word does clearly indicate its reality. St. Paul, for example, teaches the oneness of God when he says, "The grace of the Lord Jesus Christ, the love of God, and the communion of the Holy Spirit be with all of you" (2 Corinthians 13:13). Again, Paul implies the blessed Trinity when he writes, "Now there are varieties of gifts, but the same Spirit; and there are varieties of services, but the same Lord; and there are varieties of activities, but it is the same God who activates all of them in everyone"

(1 Corinthians 12:4-6). And consider these words of Christ, "When the Advocate comes, whom I will send to you from the Father, the Spirit of truth who comes from the Father, he will testify on my behalf" (John 15:26).

Why should we even *try* to understand what we can about the Trinity? Because just as Faustina did, the more we get to know God, the more we will love him: "The more I come to know Him, the more ardently, the more fiercely I love Him, and the more perfect my acts become."[14] As we grow in our love for God, we will be more willing to trust and obey him, which will bring us happiness in this life as well as throughout all eternity. This present life prepares us for the joys of heaven, where we will no longer have to use our reason and faith to draw closer to the Trinity but where we will share God's own happiness and "be like him, for we shall see him as he is" (1 John 3:2).

❧ Meditate on the reality of the blessed Trinity, and then write on a sheet of paper or in your journal your own analogy that will help you better understand the triune God. For example, recalling your childhood family, consider how the communion within its members reflected—and still reflects—the eternal communion of the Father, Son, and Holy Spirit.

❧ Consider how much time during a given week you spend thinking about God and contemplating his trinitarian being.

Toward the end of her life, when Sr. Faustina lay ill in a hospital bed, she could hear the loud voices of patients in the men's ward near her room. She could not help overhearing their conversations, which she sadly noted were never about God. In a silent prayer to Jesus, she mourned the fact that the entire world interests people, yet they spend so little time—if any at all—thinking about God. How might you carve out at least a few minutes each morning and evening to get to know better the Father, Son, and Holy Spirit? Promise yourself that by God's grace, you will begin tomorrow to do so.

❧ During or immediately following reception of Christ's body and blood in the Eucharist, the Trinity would often immerse Faustina in its reality. Though her mind could not understand God's triune nature, her soul seemed to understand, and that was enough for her. Just before you next receive holy Communion, ask Jesus to give you an inner awareness, deep within your soul where God dwells, of the reality of the Trinity. Ask the Lord, while he gives you this awareness, to help you to grow in your love for him.

❧ Sing the fourth verse of the familiar hymn "Holy God, We Praise Thy Name." As you do, let its truths seep into your heart, mind, and soul, bringing you joy and peace and helping you to rest in the loving embrace of the blessed Trinity:

Holy Father, Holy Son,
Holy Spirit, Three we name Thee;
While in essence only One,
Undivided God we claim Thee;
And adoring bend the knee,
While we own the mystery.
And adoring bend the knee,
While we own the mystery.[15]

❧ Faustina saw the oneness of God represented as an intense light that she could not approach. Within that great light, she perceived three separate light sources, which we can assume represented the three divine persons of the Trinity, manifesting their eternal reality as the one triune God. Light a candle in thanksgiving for the light in your life, the eternal Light that dwells in your soul. Whenever you are going through a dark period in your life, light a candle, and meditate on these words of Jesus: "I have come as light into the world, so that everyone who believes in me should not remain in the darkness" (John 12:46).

God's Word

"When the Advocate comes, whom I will send to you from the Father, the Spirit of truth who comes from the Father, he will testify on my behalf. You also are to testify because you have been with me from the beginning." (John 15:26-27)

There is one body and one Spirit, just as you were called to the one hope of your calling, one Lord, one faith, one baptism, one God and Father of all, who is above all and through all and in all. (Ephesians 4:4-6)

"Go therefore and make disciples of all nations, baptizing them in the name of the Father and of the Son and of the Holy Spirit, and teaching them to obey everything that I have commanded you. And remember, I am with you always, to the end of the age." (Matthew 28:19-20)

Closing Prayer: O blessed Trinity, one indivisible eternal God, my soul longs to know you as you truly are, in all your fullness. The thought that I will one day see you face to face in heaven makes my spirit sing for joy. I give you my heart, soul, mind, and body, my past, present, and future. Help me to come to know you as well as I can on earth, so that my love for you grows ever stronger. Unite me to yourself so that I may live and die in you and spend eternity singing your praises.

1. *Diary of Saint Maria Faustina Kowalska: Divine Mercy in My Soul* (Stockbridge, MA: Marians of the Immaculate Conception, 1987), 734.

2. *Diary*, 30.
3. *Diary*, 30.
4. *Diary*, 30.
5. *Diary*, 30.
6. *Diary*, 30.
7. *Diary*, 30.
8. United States Catholic Conference, *Catechism of the Catholic Church, Second Edition* (Libreria Editrice Vaticana: United States Catholic Conference, Inc., 1997), 230.
9. *Diary*, 472.
10. *Diary*, 472.
11. *Diary*, 1439.
12. *Diary*, 392.
13. *Catechism of the Catholic Church*, 2205.
14. *Diary*, 231.
15. Words attributed to Ignaz Franz, in Maria Theresa's *Katholisches Gesangbuch* (Vienna: circa 1774) (Grosser Gott, wir loben Dich). Translated from German to English by Clarence A. Walworth, 1858.

Meditation Eight

Road to Sanctification: Suffering

Theme: Suffering became prayer for Faustina. She willingly offered all her pains and trials to Jesus. She asked him to unite her sufferings with his for the salvation of souls, as well as for her own sanctification.

Opening Prayer: Dear Jesus, no matter what I do, each day offers me its own share of suffering. Lord, you know when I suffer: when people condemn, scorn, or mock me and fail to understand me; when my body complains of aches and pains; when worries cloud my mind; when my heart and soul seem void of love and faith. In those times, give me strength to contemplate your sacred head crowned with thorns and your beautiful face covered with your precious blood. Help me to imitate your selfless love by offering my own suffering as prayer for your people, the body of Christ, as well as for my own sanctification.

About Faustina

Suffering haunted Sr. Faustina throughout the entire thirteen years of her convent life. The tuberculosis that relentlessly gnawed at her lungs, bones, and entire body caused her such intense pain that toward the end of her life, she often could not sleep. Her chronic illness sapped her strength to the point where she often could not even eat or drink. Yet she did not demand a cure from Jesus; she resigned herself to whatever God willed for her. In December 1936, she wrote, "I do not desire a return to health more than death. I entrust myself completely to His infinite mercy and, as a little child, I am living in the greatest peace."[1]

Throughout most of her years with the Congregation of the Sisters of Our Lady of Mercy, only her doctors, priests, and religious superiors knew of the bodily tortures that Faustina suffered. Fewer still knew of her intense spiritual, moral, and emotional sufferings, especially in regard to the mission that Jesus gave her.

Alone in her convent cell on the evening of February 21, 1931, after working all day in the convent bakery, Jesus appeared to her. Wearing a long white garment, he raised one hand, as if bestowing a blessing. He touched his other hand to a place on his garment above his heart, and from that area two large rays burst forth, one red and one colorless, both as if transparent. Awed, Faustina gazed at Jesus in silence, her soul filled with joy. He spoke and told her to paint a picture of this image of him and to write at the bottom of the painting, *Jezu, Ufam Tobie*, "Jesus, I trust in You." He promised her that he would protect throughout life and death anyone who venerated the image. When Faustina told her confessor about the vision, he insisted that Jesus only meant that she was to paint the image on her soul, not on canvas. Wondering what to do next, she left the confessional. Then she heard Jesus speak to her soul, saying that the image was *already* on her soul and that now it had to be painted on canvas.

When Faustina related her vision to her superior, Mother Rose Klobukowska, she told Faustina to ask Jesus for a sign to prove that his appearance, as well as his subsequent demands, were not fabrications of the young nun's imagination. Later, when Faustina explained the mother superior's request to Jesus, he told her that the only sign would be the graces people would obtain from him when they venerated the Divine Mercy image. Now distressed, knowing that the mother superior would never believe her, Faustina tried to ignore the mission that Jesus had assigned to her.

Seeking relief for her conflicted conscience, Faustina spoke with her confessor, Fr. Joseph Andrasz, asking him to release her from the duty of carrying out the Lord's demands. Father's answer surely surprised her: he refused to dispense her from anything, including painting the image of the Divine Mercy. Fr. Andrasz also advised her to obtain a spiritual director to whom she could confide everything that was happening in her soul. Those orders only increased Faustina's interior suffering, and she begged Jesus to give his mission to someone else, saying, "Do not entrust such great things to me, as You see that I am a bit of dust and completely inept."[2]

When Jesus failed to release her from her mission, Faustina asked some fellow sisters if they would paint the Divine Mercy image. Finding no one willing to do it, Faustina tried to paint it herself. But her lack of artistic talent soon convinced her that someone else would have to paint it. By then rumors about her "supposed" visions of God consumed much of the conversation buzzing throughout the convent. Many sisters believed she suffered from mental illness and that her mind had deceived her. Some even thought she was "possessed by the evil spirit."[3] One of the sisters told her that she should defend herself, but Faustina "resolved to bear everything in silence and to give no explanations."[4] She knew God would give her the strength she needed to bear any sufferings he permitted.

One day one of the older superiors verbally attacked Faustina, ranting about how the Lord would never commune with "such a miserable bundle of imperfections."[5] Faustina humbly agreed with the nun and later told Jesus that she was indeed unqualified to fulfill the mission he had assigned to her. But Jesus assured her that he desired to work through weak souls like herself to accomplish his will. And work through her he did!

After making her perpetual vows in Krakow on May 1, 1933, Faustina left for her new assignment in Vilnius, where she was assigned to work as the convent gardener. While there, she met her new spiritual director, Msgr. Michael Sopocko, and in confession told him all about the mission Jesus had given her. Soon this priest became one of Faustina's greatest supporters in the work Jesus had called her to do. In fact, it was Msgr. Sopocko who ordered her to begin keeping a diary to record her encounters with God. Today the printed edition of that diary, numbering more than six hundred pages, is read by millions throughout the world.

In June 1934, after much effort and heartache on the part of Sr. Faustina, Msgr. Sopocko commissioned artist Eugene Kazimirowski to complete the painting of the Divine Mercy image. The devotion to the Divine Mercy began to spread throughout eastern Europe shortly before Faustina's death in 1938 and continued to spread after that time. However, in March 1959, the Holy See—due to a grave misunderstanding—banned the practice of the Divine Mercy Devotion as promoted in Faustina's diary. Not until April 1978, primarily at the insistence of Cardinal Archbishop Karol Wojtyla of Krakow (soon to become Pope John Paul II), did the Holy See reverse its ban. Today, because of the sacrifices of Faustina and those who followed in her footsteps, the devotion is practiced throughout the world, drawing down God's mercy upon all.

Pause: Reflect on some of the hardships you have endured. Consider how bearing your daily cross has helped you grow in holiness and grow closer to God.

Faustina's Words

I was happy to suffer for God and for the souls that have been granted His mercy during these days. Seeing that so many souls have been granted divine mercy these days, I regard as nothing even the greatest suffering and toil, even if they were to continue till the end of the world; for they will come to an end, while these souls have been saved from torments that are without end.[6]

God often grants many and great graces out of regard for the souls who are suffering, and He withholds many punishments solely because of the suffering souls.[7]

When a soul has come out of these tribulations, it is deeply humble. Its purity of soul is great. . . . The soul has been purified by God himself.[8]

Reflection

God assures us that even our greatest sufferings are nothing compared to the happiness of heaven that awaits us if we persevere (Romans 8:18). But how can we persevere when our trials—whether physical, emotional, or spiritual—seem at times unbearable? When we watch helplessly, for instance, as a loved one suffers, how can we bear the tormenting pain in our heart and soul? In the middle of our suffering, we often ask if God has deserted us. If he loves us and sees everything happening to us, why does he allow us and those we love to suffer? Scripture assures us that God can bring good out of even the worst circumstances (Romans 8:28). Clinging to God's promises when we suffer can mean the difference between hope and despair.

Does God actually have a purpose for our suffering? St. Paul discovered that when we undergo afflictions in union with Christ's sufferings, God comforts us so that we in turn can comfort others in their suffering (2 Corinthians 1:4-7). Jesus tells us that if we persevere in our sufferings, if we do not give up under the weight of our daily crosses, we will be saved (Matthew 10:22). Faustina embraced suffering not only for her own sanctification but for that of others as well. She even rejoiced in her sufferings because she believed that somehow God would use her afflictions to save souls (Colossians 1:24).

Jesus tells us that we should even "take courage" in the face of trials and tribulations because he has already overcome the world (John 16:33). When St. Paul complained to him about a particular trial he was undergoing and begged Jesus to relieve him of it, the Lord refused, saying that in Paul's very weakness lay God's strength. Instead of questioning God, Paul declared that he would embrace his weaknesses and sufferings and even boast of them so that Christ's power would manifest itself through them: "Therefore I am content with weaknesses, insults, hardships, persecutions, and calamities for the sake of Christ; for whenever I am weak, then I am strong" (2 Corinthians 12:10). We can welcome God's assurance that nothing can separate us from Christ's love and that through him we will ultimately triumph—if we but rely on his strength and not ours (Romans 8:28-39).

When you feel, like Faustina, that you are too weak and inept to successfully bear a certain trial or to fulfill a task you believe God has given you, find a quiet spot where you can sit down by yourself for five minutes. Close your eyes, and breathe deeply several times, allowing your mind and body to release all anxiety and tension. Imagine Jesus sitting beside you, gently embracing you and saying, "Don't worry. You never need to rely on your own limited strength in the face of any seemingly insurmountable challenge. *Because* you are weak and finite, I can work through you, and my strength will lead you to victory."

Often when Faustina suffered, she took refuge in the "Heart of Him who alone understands what pain and suffering is."[9] When afflicted, try one of her favorite sources of comfort: imagine yourself tucked into the tabernacle next to Jesus' body and blood, resting your head on his heart, confiding to him all your troubles and even shedding tears if you feel the need.[10] Recall how Jesus, during his agony in the garden, cried out to God, "My Father, if it is possible, let this cup pass from me." Take the next step with Jesus, and say, "Yet not what I want but what you want" (Matthew 26:39), and experience God's peace.

❧ As an examination of conscience, ask yourself these questions: How do my afflictions affect my faith? Do I trust God to cause something good to come out of even the worst events and problems in my life? Does suffering cause me to close myself off from others, depriving them of the blessing of helping me? What crosses does God seem to be calling me to embrace? Have I consistently reached out to others in their suffering?

Then ask God to forgive you for any wrongdoing or lack of faith. Ask for the grace to trust him, no matter what difficulty you face.

❧ When your difficulties seem to block out the reality of God's presence, recall this scriptural truth: "God is our refuge and strength, a very present help in trouble" (Psalm 46:1). Then, in prayer, imagine that the Lord is standing at your side, right at the very moment when you most need him, there to shelter you from any oncoming storms.

❧ Though it seems opposite to what the world tells you, the next time suffering afflicts you, challenge yourself to follow Paul's advice: "Rejoice always, pray without ceasing, give thanks in all circumstances; for this is the will of God in Christ Jesus for you" (1 Thessalonians 5:16-18). Ask the Holy Spirit to help you to continue in this attitude of joyful prayer and thanksgiving whenever you are enduring trials and suffering.

God's Word

We also boast in our sufferings, knowing that suffering produces endurance, and endurance produces character, and character produces hope, and hope does not disappoint us, because God's love has been poured into our hearts through the Holy Spirit that has been given to us. (Romans 5:3-5)

I am now rejoicing in my sufferings for your sake, and in my flesh I am completing what is lacking in Christ's afflictions for the sake of his body, that is, the church. (Colossians 1:24)

Closing Prayer: My Lord Jesus, I know that my sufferings help to make me more like you. In the face of my weaknesses, help me to rely on your strength. Use my trials to draw me ever closer to you in humility and love. I will trust that even my darkest misery cannot separate me from you.

1. *Diary of Saint Maria Faustina Kowalska: Divine Mercy in My Soul* (Stockbridge, MA: Marians of the Immaculate Conception, 1987), 795.
2. *Diary*, 53.
3. *Diary*, 133.
4. *Diary*, 126.
5. *Diary*, 133.
6. *Diary*, 421.
7. *Diary*, 1268.

8. *Diary*, 115.
9. *Diary*, 1454.
10. *Diary*, 1454.

Meditation Nine

To Thee Do I Pray

Theme: Sr. Faustina used every opportunity to pray. She learned to remain in God's presence, no matter where she was or what she was doing, and to yield her soul to the Holy Spirit, so that always and everywhere he could pray and intercede through her. She prayed not only for the living but for the souls in purgatory. And in imitation of St. Paul, she tried to "give thanks in all circumstances" (1 Thessalonians 5:18), whether those "circumstances" brought joy or pain.

Opening Prayer: Father, my only hope is in you, so why don't I spend every moment praying, if not with my mind and lips, then with my spirit and my soul? Jesus, Son of God, who deserves all my praise, why doesn't my heart show its gratitude by giving you constant thanks? Holy Spirit, dwelling within my soul, since I don't even know *how* to pray as I should, please pray continuously through my mind, heart, soul, and body, interceding for me and giving thanks and praise, always and everywhere, to you.

About Faustina

One day in 1937, after receiving the body and blood of Christ in holy Communion, Sr. Faustina went to her cell to offer to God a "long act of thanksgiving."[1] Faustina gazed lovingly at the crucified corpus of her Lord on the wooden cross hanging on the wall above her narrow bed and began to thank and praise him for coming to her. At that moment, Faustina experienced light—*the* Light who is Jesus (John 8:12)—flooding her soul, nourishing it with his love. Overcome by her own immense love for him, she lay face down on the floor, barely noticing its cold, hard surface.

What did Jesus want to say to her? Or did he want her to merely enjoy these moments of "purely spiritual union with God"? In answer to her questions, a new flood of light pierced her "through and through," and as she yielded her mind, heart, and soul to it, Jesus began to remind her of all the graces he had been "constantly lavishing" upon her.[2] One of those graces was the gift of prayer in all its forms. And she knew well that without the Holy Spirit dwelling within her, in her weakness she would never be able to pray as she "ought" (Romans 8:26).

Still facedown on the hard floor, Sr. Faustina now allowed the Spirit of God to pray through her "with sighs too deep for words" (Romans 8:26). As her heart poured out its gratitude for all the inconceivable favors God had given her—and now promised to continue to give her—Faustina's eyes overflowed with tears. Surely Jesus would accept her tears as prayers, too, and allow her to bathe his feet with her tears as did the sinful woman at the home of the Pharisee (Luke 7:37-38).

How long Sr. Faustina remained in tearful prayer, she did not know, but when she finally tried to stand up, new light pierced her soul and prevented her from rising. On her third attempt, she succeeded in standing, and from there Christ lifted her up into the tender embrace of his heart, where she knew, without a doubt, that "God alone" was "enough" for her.[3]

The next day, the profound gratitude Sr. Faustina still felt toward God for all that he had shown her the day before flowed from her heart and onto the pages of her diary in the form of a poem. In the beginning of that poem, which she offered to Jesus as a prayer, she thanked him for all the graces he lavished upon her, "graces which enlighten me with the brilliance of the sun."[4]

Pause: Consider inviting the Holy Spirit to help you to "pray without ceasing" and to "give thanks in all circumstances" (1 Thessalonians 5:17-18).

Faustina's Words

Thank You, O Holy Trinity, for the vastness of the graces
Which You have lavished on me unceasingly through life.
My gratitude will intensify as the eternal dawn rises,
When, for the first time, I sing to Your glory.[5]

My Jesus, I am going into the wilderness today to speak only with You, my Master and my Lord. Let the earth be silent, and You alone speak to me, Jesus. You know that I understand no other voice but Yours, O Good Shepherd. In the dwelling of my heart is that wilderness to which no creature has access. There, You alone are King.[6]

A soul arms itself by prayer for all kinds of combat. In whatever state the soul may be, it ought to pray. A soul which is pure and beautiful must pray, or else it will lose its beauty; a soul which is striving after this purity must pray, or else it will never attain it; a soul which is newly converted must pray, or else it will fall again; a sinful soul, plunged in sins, must pray so that it might rise again. There is no soul which is not bound to pray, for every single grace comes to the soul through prayer.[7]

There are times in life when the soul finds comfort only in profound prayer. Would that souls knew how to persevere in prayer at such times. This is very important.[8]

Reflection

How should we pray? Sr. Faustina's life shows us that God accepts any type of prayer from his children—whether it be written, sung, spoken, or thought; whether our prayer is offered to God in the form of reading Scripture or performing good deeds; or whether our method of praying is simply to remain "still before the LORD" (Psalm 37:7) and wait for his loving whisper. The Lord will even accept as prayer a sudden rush of love from our heart, a quick heavenward glance, or merely the intention or desire to pray.

To get us started praying, Jesus gave us the Our Father (see Matthew 6:9-13). Then, if we humbly ask the Holy Spirit to pray through us, he will do so, just as he did through Sr. Faustina, because it is the Spirit of Jesus who "intercedes for the saints according to the will of God" (Romans 8:27), and we are those "saints." In fact, if we allow him to do so, the Holy Spirit will daily inspire us to offer up an endless variety of the five basic forms of prayer: petition, intercession, thanksgiving, blessing, and praise. Through our petitions, we ask God for what we need. We can also intercede for others, asking God to help them, too. In gratitude for all the blessings we receive, we offer God our profound thanks. And because he blesses us, we can, in turn, bless God. Finally, we can allow the Spirit to offer continual praise through us to the Lord of the universe who says, "I am the first and I am the last; besides me there is no god" (Isaiah 44:6).

When it comes to prayer, we need not ever fear making a mistake—except to not pray at all. Before praying, we simply need to remember who we are—God's beloved children—and to whom we are praying—our loving Father. With confidence as God's sons and daughters, and by the power of the Holy

Spirit, we can then cry out, as did the only begotten Son of God: "Abba! Father!" (Galatians 4:6 and Mark 14:36).

❧ From despair to joy, from anger to love, the psalms cover every basic human emotion, desire, and need. By thoughtfully reading the 150 psalms, you can allow the Holy Spirit to teach you how to pray. Beginning with Psalm 1, you could easily "pray" one psalm each night before going to sleep. As you pray each psalm, allow it to express your own deepest emotions and needs. For future reference, you could even use a pencil to mark in the margins beside each psalm what basic emotions or needs that particular psalm expresses. For example, as you read Psalm 88, you might write in the margin "loneliness, despair, fear, guilt, shame, sorrow." Three nights later, as you read Psalm 91, you might pencil in "faith, love, protection, praise, peace, joy." By the time you reach Psalm 150, you will have learned how to pray simply and spontaneously from your heart. And at the end of that last psalm, you just might find yourself wanting to shout that final "Praise the LORD!"

❧ Do you ever feel as if your prayers aren't good or important enough to please God? Faustina once felt that way, too, until the Holy Spirit helped her to understand that God welcomes even the smallest and weakest of our prayers. Just as the parent of a child who has left the "nest" longs to receive a message from that child, so, too, does God our Father long for even a nod or whisper from us. Examine your conscience to see how often you lift your heart in prayer to God, your loving Father. Determine that starting tomorrow, you will, as often as possible, lift up—silently or aloud—a quick and simple prayer such as "Jesus, I love you" or "All glory to you, Lord" or "Thank you, dear God."

❧ Meditate on the following Scripture passage: "Do not worry about anything, but in everything by prayer and supplication with thanksgiving let your requests be made known to God. And the peace of God, which surpasses all understanding, will guard your hearts and your minds in Christ Jesus" (Philippians 4:6-7). Ask the Holy Spirit to help you to always pray about anything that bothers you and then to surrender it to God's hands.

❧ Recall someone you do not like, someone whose very presence annoys you. When did you last pray for that person? Determine today to begin to pray at least once a day for him or her. It may take several days, weeks, months, or even years, but if you persevere in praying daily for that person, you may discover that the Holy Spirit has used your prayers, not to change that person, but to change your own attitude toward him or her.

❧ In 1938 before Faustina's death, a fellow sister asked her to pray for her specific needs when Faustina reached heaven. In all humility, without any presumption or pride, Sr. Faustina agreed to intercede for her and said that after her death she would be able to do more for those left on earth than she had done for them while she was alive.[9] Put your trust in Faustina's promise, and take your needs to her, asking her to intercede for you before God's throne.

God's Word

Give ear to my words, O Lord;
 give heed to my sighing.
Listen to the sound of my cry,
 my King and my God,
 for to you I pray. (Psalm 5:1-2)

Then Jesus told them a parable about their need to pray always and not to lose heart. (Luke 18:1)

The prayer of the righteous is powerful and effective. (James 5:16)

Devote yourselves to prayer, keeping alert in it with thanksgiving. (Colossians 4:2)

For the eyes of the Lord are on the righteous,
 and his ears are open to their prayer. (1 Peter 3:12)

Closing Prayer: God of mercy, forgive all my foolish prayers and "wrongful" intentions that only serve my self-love and self-interest. Holy Spirit, put your own words into my heart and mind and on my lips, so that I may always pray according to God's loving desires and not according to my own misguided ones. And Lord, remind me to always thank you for everything, even when you do not answer my prayers in the way I would prefer.

1. *Diary of Saint Maria Faustina Kowalska: Divine Mercy in My Soul* (Stockbridge, MA: Marians of the Immaculate Conception, 1987), 1279.
2. *Diary,* 1278.
3. *Diary,* 1279.
4. *Diary,* 1286.
5. *Diary,* 1286.
6. *Diary,* 725.
7. *Diary*, 146.
8. *Diary*, 860.
9. *Diary*, 1614.

Meditation Ten

The Blessed Sacrament

Theme: Faustina frequently meditated before Christ's real presence in the tabernacle. When she could not physically visit the Eucharist, she spiritually placed herself before the tabernacle. She believed that in the Blessed Sacrament lay the "whole secret"[1] of her sanctity.

Opening Prayer: Lord Jesus, when I receive you in the Eucharist, help me to meditate on and adore your real presence within me. When I cannot receive you sacramentally, remind me to place myself before you in the tabernacle so that, by the power of your Holy Spirit, I can receive you in spirit.

About Faustina

Believing with all her heart that everything good within her was "due to Holy Communion,"[2] Faustina made every attempt to receive her Lord in the Eucharist. Even toward the end of her thirty-three years, suffering from tuberculosis, she did her best to daily receive the body and blood of Jesus.

Lying ill on her bed in the isolation ward of the tuberculosis sanatorium in Krakow on January 10, 1937, Sr. Faustina begged the Lord to give her enough strength the next morning to trudge down the stairs and into the chapel to receive his body and blood. She said to him, "You see very well, Jesus, that here they do not bring Holy Communion to the sick; so, if You do not strengthen me for that moment so that I can go down to the chapel, how can I receive You in the Mystery of Love?"[3]

The following morning the Lord answered Faustina's prayer by giving her just enough strength to successfully negotiate the stairs to the sanatorium chapel, to receive the Eucharist, and then to slowly return upstairs to her bed. "But as soon as I returned from the chapel, all the sufferings and weaknesses immediately returned, as if they had been waiting for me," she wrote.[4] This did not disturb her; as she explained in her diary, she did not fear suffering, because "the Bread of the Strong"[5] had given her inner strength to peacefully and willingly bear her afflictions. Calling Christ's real presence in the consecrated host her "sweet Master and faithful Friend,"[6] Faustina wrote of her happiness in knowing that Jesus remained always within her. Even in the sanatorium's isolation ward, loneliness did not plague her, because as she later wrote, "Jesus-Host, we know each other—and that is enough for me."[7]

Two days later, on January 12, when Dr. Adam Silberg examined Sr. Faustina in her isolation room, her high fever worried him. He told her to take her temperature every morning before Mass. If it was not normal, he said, she should not go down to the chapel. Even though this decree grieved Faustina, she quietly consented to Dr. Silberg's orders. She knew that Jesus always wanted her to obey her doctors, superiors, and priests, as if he himself were speaking through them.

That evening, lamenting the possibility that she might have to miss Communion for many days until her temperature dropped, Faustina asked Jesus to make her temperature normal the following morning so that she could receive him. The next morning, her prayer was answered. When Dr. Silberg visited her that day and she told him that she had no fever, he was amazed. She begged the doctor to not make it difficult for her to receive Communion each morning in the chapel, pointing out that not receiving Jesus in the Eucharist would have an adverse effect on her treatment. The doctor replied that if the weather was favorable on any given morning, and if the frail Sr. Faustina felt well enough to do so, she could go to the chapel for Communion.

After the doctor left her room that day, Faustina told Jesus, "I have already done whatever was up to me; now I am counting on You and am quite at peace."[8]

Pause: Reflect on your own belief about and devotion to Christ's real presence in the Eucharist.

Faustina's Words

All the good that is in me is due to Holy Communion. I owe everything to it. I feel that this holy fire has transformed me completely. Oh, how happy I am to be a dwelling place for You, O Lord! My heart is a temple in which You dwell continually. . . .[9]

All the strength of my soul flows from the Blessed Sacrament. I spend all my free moments in conversation with Him. He is my Master.[10]

O Lamb of God, I do not know what to admire in You first: Your gentleness, Your hidden life, the emptying of Yourself for the sake of man, or the constant miracle of Your mercy [the Eucharist], which transforms souls and raises them up to eternal life.[11]

Reflection

The Church has always believed in and defended the doctrine of the real presence of Christ in the Eucharist.[12] Christ instituted the Eucharist at the Last Supper and later commissioned his apostles to continue his ministry by giving them the gift of the Holy Spirit. "As the Father has sent me, so I send you" (John 20:21). In turn, the apostles ordained and commissioned bishops to continue Christ's mission. This very same process of commissioning and ordaining has continued uninterrupted and will continue until the end of time. That unbroken connection between the apostles and today's ordained priests is called "apostolic succession."[13]

To priests is given the gift of consecrating ordinary bread and wine into the body and blood of Christ. Apostolic succession assures us that the Eucharist we receive truly is the real presence of our Lord Jesus Christ—body, blood, soul, and divinity.

Today and every day, Jesus invites us to follow St. Faustina's example and receive strength to lead sanctified lives from our reception of the Eucharist. Faustina wrote in her diary that if she did not receive our Lord in the Eucharist, she would "fall continually." Just as she received all her "comfort" from holy Communion, we can, too, and we can declare along with her, "Jesus concealed in the Host is everything to me. From the tabernacle I draw strength, power, courage, and light. I would not know how to give glory to God if I did not have the Eucharist in my heart."[14]

❧ Carve out some time in the next day or two to reflect on the following questions: When I receive the Eucharist, do I expect nourishment for my soul? How strong is my devotion to the real presence of Christ in the Blessed Sacrament? Might I strengthen my devotion by attending daily Mass or by frequently visiting the local parish church and adoring Christ's real presence in the tabernacle?

❧ Each time you receive Jesus in the Blessed Sacrament, examine your conscience to make sure you do not receive him unworthily. Ask the Holy Spirit to help you search your heart and convict you of any wrongdoing. Ask the Lord for forgiveness for your sins, and then say an Act of Contrition. For serious sin, seek absolution from a priest in the Sacrament of Reconciliation.

❧ The Old Testament prefigures the Eucharist in passages such as Exodus 12:1-3 and 12:21-28. Read these passages, and ponder their meaning for you and for the body of Christ, the Church. Then meditate on any or all of the passages in the New Testament that pertain to the Eucharist, such as Mark 14:22-25, 1 Corinthians 11:23-32, and Luke 24:30-35. Make an act of thanksgiving to the Lord for giving you so great a gift.

❧ During March 1938, Sr. Faustina offered every Mass she attended and every Eucharist she received for her priest, Fr. Andrasz, "asking God to give him an even deeper understanding of His love and mercy."[15] Consider offering your next Mass and Communion to God for your own pastor. Offer each succeeding Mass and Communion for a different individual from among your family and friends.

❧ Find a quiet spot where you can, undisturbed, reread the first quotation under "Faustina's Words." Close your eyes, breathe deeply until your body and mind relax, and then meditate on the fact that because you have—at some point in your life, if not within the last week—received Christ in the Eucharist, his gentle and loving "holy fire" dwells within you. Ask him to continually transform you into the person he wants you to be, and then allow your soul to silently worship him.

God's Word

[Jesus said,] "I am the bread of life. Your ancestors ate the manna in the wilderness, and they died. This is the bread that comes down from heaven, so that one may eat of it and not die. I am the living bread that came down from heaven. Whoever eats of this bread will live forever; and the bread that I will give for the life of the world is my flesh." (John 6:48-51)

So Jesus said to them, "Very truly, I tell you, unless you eat the flesh of the Son of Man and drink his blood, you have no life in you. Those who eat my flesh and drink my blood have eternal life, and I will raise them up on the last day; for my flesh is true food and my blood is true drink. Those who eat my flesh and drink my blood abide in me, and I in them. Just as the living Father sent me, and I live because of the Father, so whoever eats me will live because of me. This is the bread that came down from heaven, not like that which your ancestors ate, and they died. But the one who eats this bread will live forever." (John 6:53-58)

Closing Prayer: Jesus, I have no words that can adequately express to you my gratitude for what you have sacrificed—and continue to sacrifice—so that I might receive your body, blood, soul, and divinity in the Eucharist. The thought of your profound love and humility in choosing to hide your eternal self within the finite elements of bread and wine overwhelms me. By the power of your Holy Spirit, Lord, help me to grow in my devotion to you in the Blessed Sacrament.

1. *Diary of Saint Maria Faustina Kowalska: Divine Mercy in My Soul* (Stockbridge, MA: Marians of the Immaculate Conception, 1987), 1489.
2. *Diary*, 1392.
3. *Diary*, 876.
4. *Diary*, 876.
5. *Diary*, 876.
6. *Diary*, 877.
7. *Diary*, 877.
8. *Diary*, 878.
9. *Diary*, 1392.
10. *Diary*, 1404.
11. *Diary*, 1584.
12. United States Catholic Conference, *Catechism of the Catholic Church, Second Edition* (Libreria Editrice Vaticana: United States Catholic Conference, Inc., 1997), 1357.
13. Peter M. J. Stravinskas, ed., *Our Sunday Visitor's Catholic Encyclopedia, Revised Edition* (Huntington, Indiana: Our Sunday Visitor Publishing Division, 1998), 95.
14. *Diary*, 1037.
15. *Diary*, 1623.

Meditation Eleven

That Heavenly Homeland

Theme: Her visions of heaven, purgatory, and hell helped to fuel and form Sr. Faustina's lifelong desire to lead a holy, saintly life and to spend her eternity in that glorious, heavenly homeland to which God has called all people.

Opening Prayer: Oh Lord, grant me the grace to imitate the saints' virtues just as they imitated yours, so that one day I will join them in heaven to love and praise you throughout eternity. Make my desire for heaven so strong that it melts away any fears I have of death.

About Faustina

During her convent years, God graced Faustina with visions of heaven, hell, and purgatory. Four years before her death in 1938,[1] Jesus commanded her to record in her diary all the spiritual experiences, insights, and visions he would share with her. Often he reminded her that she was to do this, not for herself, but for the sake of all who would read or hear about her words. On January 23, 1937, for example, she wrote that she did not feel like writing that day. Moments later Jesus told her, "My daughter, you do not live for yourself but for souls; write for their benefit."[2] So, until shortly before her death, she wrote during every free moment she could squeeze out of the convent's demanding schedule.

One of the most painful events Faustina wrote about was her vision of hell, which she experienced during an eight-day retreat in October 1936.[3] The sight of the torments of the souls eternally consigned to that dark place, with its "terrible suffocating smell," grieved Faustina. However, obedient as always to Jesus, she wrote about it "so that no soul may find an excuse by saying there is no hell, or that nobody has ever been there, and so no one can say what it is like."[4] That frightening vision of hell motivated Faustina to pray even more fervently and frequently for sinners so that they would realize that no matter how many and great their sins, Jesus longed for them to seek refuge in his merciful, loving heart. She knew that even the greatest of sinners[5] would find forgiveness, healing, peace, and joy there.

On many occasions during her convent years, Sr. Faustina also experienced visions of purgatory. Jesus wanted her to fully recognize that though the souls being purified there would one day enter the joys of heaven, they still had great need of her prayers. One evening in August 1925, Faustina, led by her guardian angel, saw how the souls in purgatory unceasingly prayed for themselves but without any positive results. Realizing that only God's people still on earth could effectively pray for them, Faustina intensified her prayers for the souls in purgatory and by writing in her diary about her vision, she encouraged everyone to pray for them, too.

Though Jesus showed Faustina hell and purgatory, he also allowed her many glimpses of heaven, which served to increase her determination to spread his message of love and mercy to the world. Her experiences of heaven helped her persevere in holiness so that she could one day join the saints there to worship and love the God of mercy. By writing in her diary about these experiences, she knew the Lord would use them to encourage other souls, too, to continue to strive for holiness.

On November 27, 1936, in bed suffering from tuberculosis, Faustina struggled to record in her diary a vision she had experienced earlier that day: "Today, I was in heaven in spirit, and I saw its inconceivable beauties and the happiness that awaits us after death."[6] As she continued to write, she revealed how she had witnessed all those in heaven contemplating God, the source of their endless joy, and how this joy caused them to praise and glorify him. She saw the unchanging, eternal majesty of God worshipped by the "heavenly spirits."[7] This incredible sight filled her with peace, love, and joy as she realized anew how insignificant she was compared to the greatness of God, and she rejoiced in that realization because "since I am little, He carries me in His arms and holds me close to His Heart."[8]

Through this vision, God helped Faustina understand that what he values the most in people is love. Nothing compares in his eyes to even the smallest act of love. And when a person shows sincere love, God "gifts" that soul with "inconceivable favors."[9] This vision convinced her of the truth of this Scripture: "No eye has seen, nor ear heard, nor the human heart conceived, what God has prepared for those who love him" (1 Corinthians 2:9). And this, in turn, inspired her to promise to pray more fervently for all the people who did not believe in life after death. She would, all her remaining days, beg God to envelop them with his mercy and "clasp them to His fatherly bosom."[10]

Pause: Take an honest look at your own beliefs about eternal life.

Faustina's Words

Damnation is for the soul who wants to be damned; but for the one who desires salvation, there is the inexhaustible ocean of the Lord's mercy to draw from.[11]

Eternity! Who can understand this one word which comes from You, O incomprehensible God, this one word: eternity![12]

I know that God is my ultimate goal and so, in whatever I undertake, I take God into account.[13]

During meditation, the Lord gave me knowledge of the joy of heaven and of the saints on our arrival there; they love God as the sole object of their love, but they also have a tender and heartfelt love for us. It is from the face of God that this joy flows out upon all, because we see Him face to face. His face is so sweet that the soul falls anew into ecstasy.[14]

Reflection

We are skilled at avoiding the topic of death and dying, but since dying is an inevitable part of life, our discussing, meditating on, and accepting its inevitability can help us focus our lives on God and heaven, our ultimate goal. Living each day as if it might be our last can help us follow Christ's example of holiness and love. After all, that is God's will for us, and he longs to help us do exactly that by filling us with his Holy Spirit. Faustina knew all these truths and clung to Jesus as her only hope and source of salvation, which indeed he is for all of us.

Through his death and resurrection, Jesus made possible our own resurrection into the eternal joys of heaven, if we live our lives in obedience to his will. But with evil waiting for us around every corner, how can we lead holy lives? When we look at Faustina's life, we might mistakenly think her holiness was totally her own doing. But she admitted that her sanctity was due totally to God's mercy and grace. "In spite of my wretchedness, I want to become a saint, and I trust that God's mercy can make a saint even out of such misery as I am."[15] There lies the answer for each of us. All we need to do is to *want* to lead holy lives and then to ask God to help us do so, for what is impossible for us to achieve on our own, God can do through us. When Jesus told a group of people that "it is easier for a camel to go through the eye of a needle than for someone who is rich to enter the kingdom of God," they asked, "Then who can be saved?" Jesus replied, "What is impossible for mortals is possible for God" (Luke 18:25-26).

Many people are afraid of death because it will take them away from the world they know into the unknown. Others may fear what might happen to them if they die without repenting of a particular sin. Boldly look at death. What attitude do you usually have toward it? Consider what might make you fearful. Ask the Lord to help you break free of any habitual sin and to overcome any fears you might harbor of dying.

Read the Scripture passages in "God's Word" on pp. 26–27. Note which ones touch your heart the most, the ones that help you replace your fear of death with confidence in divine providence. Call those Scriptures to mind whenever you find yourself fearing death.

The next time you attend a funeral Mass, carefully listen to all that the priest and other speakers say about death and the person who has just died. If music is sung during the service, be attentive to the words, and allow the power of the music to seep into your heart, mind, and soul, replacing your fear of death with God's love, peace, and assurance.

❧ Recall Christ's crucifixion and how one of the criminals crucified beside him pleaded, "Jesus, remember me when you come into your kingdom," and how Jesus replied, "Truly I tell you, today you will be with me in Paradise" (Luke 23:42-43). Meditate on that one word: "paradise." What does it mean to you? On a sheet of paper or in your journal, list what conditions, people, and opportunities—even if they seem foolish—you would like to find when you get to heaven. When you finish your list, offer it to God, recalling that "no eye has seen, nor ear heard, nor the human heart conceived, what God has prepared for those who love him" (1 Corinthians 2:9). Then smile at Jesus and say, "I know that my most magnificent imaginings of what heaven will be like do not even come close to the true glory, beauty, and joy of what you, dear Lord, have prepared for me."

❧ Consider the virtuous life of Faustina. In what ways did she demonstrate holiness, whether through her actions or written words? How might you emulate her? Ask her to intercede for you to Jesus for the graces and perseverance you need to reach heaven when you die.

On a sheet of paper or in your journal, write your own epitaph, recording how you would like to be remembered after death. Ask Jesus to help you always live up to your expectations of yourself and your life.

God's Word

And just as it is appointed for mortals to die once, and after that the judgment, so Christ, having been offered once to bear the sins of many, will appear a second time, not to deal with sin, but to save those who are eagerly waiting for him. (Hebrews 9:27-28)

Then I saw a new heaven and a new earth; for the first heaven and the first earth had passed away, and the sea was no more. And I saw the holy city, the new Jerusalem, coming down out of heaven from God, prepared as a bride adorned for her husband. And I heard a loud voice from the throne saying,

"See, the home of God is among mortals.
He will dwell with them;
they will be his peoples,
and God himself will be with them;
he will wipe every tear from their eyes.
Death will be no more;
mourning and crying and pain will be no more,

for the first things have passed away."
(Revelation 21:1-4)

Closing Prayer: Oh God, help me to live each day as if it might be the very day you have chosen to escort me from this world into eternity. Prepare me, Lord, for that final moment of my life, leading me always along "right paths" (Psalms 23:3). Help me to believe that even though on my own I can never reach that heavenly homeland to which you have called me, by your grace, love, and mercy I can—and will—do so.

1. *Diary of Saint Maria Faustina Kowalska: Divine Mercy in My Soul* (Stockbridge, MA: Marians of the Immaculate Conception, 1987), 6.
2. *Diary,* 895.
3. Sophia Michalenko, *Mercy My Mission* (Stockbridge, MA: Congregation of Marians, 1987), 117.
4. *Diary,* 741.
5. *Diary,* 1146.
6. *Diary*, 777.
7. *Diary*, 779.
8. *Diary*, 779.
9. *Diary*, 778.
10. *Diary*, 780.
11. *Diary*, 631.
12. *Diary*, 578.
13. *Diary*, 1329.
14. *Diary*, 1592.
15. *Diary*, 1333.

Meditation Twelve

Humility

Theme: Sr. Faustina found the secret to happiness in humility, in knowing that we are totally dependent on God and that we are "wretchedness and nothingness"[1] without him.

Opening Prayer: I want to live humbly, Jesus, always following your example, you who clothed yourself in our weak humanity in order to save us. Imprint upon my heart, soul, and mind your own humility, Lord, and help me to follow you, always aware of my own weaknesses and of the fact that without you I am nothing.

About Faustina

God blessed Faustina with many spiritual gifts, including bilocation (the ability to be in two places at one time), prophecy, reading of souls, and the invisible stigmata (painful representations of the wounds of Christ crucified). However, these gifts did not make her think more highly of herself or make her think that she was more important than others. "I know very well what I am of myself," she wrote in her diary, "because for this purpose Jesus has opened the eyes of my soul; I am an abyss of misery, and hence I understand that whatever good there is in my soul consists solely of His holy grace."[2]

But even in what we would presume to be the holy atmosphere of convent life, Faustina's humility did not go untried by opposition. In fact, in her diary she recorded numerous incidences in which her humility was tested.

In January 1938, that final bitter winter of her life, Faustina compared herself to Job. Like Faustina, Job suffered a multitude of lingering afflictions and endured many distressful setbacks and, in the process, lost the love and support of his friends and family. Like Job, the longer Faustina's illness dragged on, the less did those around her even bother to notice her suffering. As her physical pain intensified during that final year of her life, almost no one around her seemed to care; most either ignored her or took advantage of her goodwill and humility by commanding her to do undesirable, lowly tasks that they themselves did not want to do themselves.

One evening that month, as a heavy rain beat against the outside of the convent, Sr. Faustina feebly trudged down the hallway on her way back to her cell, her condition causing her tremendous pain. As she was about to pass the sister assistant, Sr. Seraphina, Faustina heard her asking another nun to go out into the storm to take a message to the convent's gatekeeper. But just then Sr. Seraphina spotted Faustina and subsequently dismissed the other nun, telling her, "No, Sister, you need not go, but Sister Faustina will, because it is raining heavily."[3]

Though Faustina was feeling so ill she did not even know if she had enough strength to drag herself back to her cell for the night, she humbly agreed to take the message to the gatekeeper. But later in her diary on January 21, she wrote that "only God knows the whole of it. This is just one example among many."[4] By "many" she meant the hundreds of incidences during her convent life when her fellow sisters and even some priests failed to act compassionately toward her, treating her with obvious disrespect and sometimes ignoring her chronic physical sufferings as if she did not deserve sympathy.

Today we would recognize some of the actions of those sisters as abusive, and we would advise the victim to speak up about her treatment. Although Faustina chose to be silent, she did not allow herself to become bitter, defensive, or vindictive. Instead, she accepted everything—good or bad—with humility. "O my Jesus," she once wrote, "nothing is better for the soul than humiliations."[5] What did she mean by that? Perhaps Faustina's humiliations helped to remind her of her own weaknesses and limitations, which were a stark contrast to God's incomparable power and majesty. Knowing that she could accomplish nothing of worth and could have no goodness within herself "without His help,"[6] Faustina found joy and peace.

Pause: Ask yourself, "Am I willing to imitate Faustina's humility by refusing to become bitter, defensive, or vengeful when I am ill-treated or criticized?"

Faustina's Words

Without humility, we cannot be pleasing to God.[7]

Nothing is difficult for the humble.[8]

My soul is drowning in the Lord, realizing the great Majesty of God and its own littleness; but through this knowledge my happiness increases. . . . This awareness is so vivid in the soul, so powerful and, at the same time, so sweet.[9]

If there is a truly happy soul upon earth, it can only be a truly humble soul.[10]

A humble soul does not trust itself, but places all its confidence in God. God defends the humble soul and lets Himself into its secrets, and the soul abides in unsurpassable happiness which no one can comprehend.[11]

Reflection

Humility, like any virtue, is a gift from God. After we ask for and receive it, we must practice it—by God's grace. In practicing humility, who should we take as our model? As Faustina did, we could follow in the footsteps of the only perfect man, Jesus. We might consider, for example, his profound humility: "Though he was in the form of God, [he] did not regard equality with God as something to be exploited, but emptied himself, taking the form of a slave, being born in human likeness" (Philippians 2:6-7). Or consider why he performed the "first of his signs" (John 2:11) at the wedding feast of Cana when he changed the water into wine. In his profound humility, he did this at the urging of his mother, even though he had at first refused, telling her, "My hour has not yet come" (John 2:4). Or consider today how he hides himself within every tabernacle under the guise of humble, ordinary bread.

Knowing by faith that in his unfathomable love for us, God will give us the grace to be humble in every situation, we can actually rejoice, like Faustina, in our weaknesses and "littleness." In recognizing, accepting, and embracing our limitations and sinfulness while at the same time growing in our awareness of the greatness of God, we practice humility. When we become "poor in spirit," our reward will be the "kingdom of heaven" (Matthew 5:3), as Jesus promises in the Beatitudes. And when we rejoice in, thank God for, and patiently bear humiliations, persecutions, and injustices, our "reward is great in heaven" (Matthew 5:11-12).

Visualize Mary, the unwed teenager pregnant with the Son of God. Imagine the unjust ridicule she may have experienced from her neighbors and relatives when they discovered she was pregnant. How do you think Mary reacted to the situation? Recall a recent incident in your own life when someone ridiculed, mocked, or unjustly judged you. How did your reaction compare with Mary's? The next time anyone criticizes you unjustly, practice humility by not becoming defensive. Instead, say a brief prayer for that person.

❧ If we lack humility, if we do not fully accept God's omnipotence and our own powerlessness before him, how can we pray effectively? According to Church teaching, "humility is the foundation of prayer."[12] Jesus tells us to imitate the tax collector, who beat on his chest while praying, "God, be merciful to me, a sinner!" (Luke 18:13). Repeat that tax collector's prayer, either aloud or silently, until the truth of your own sinfulness, weakness, and "littleness" permeates your mind, heart, and soul.

❧ Do you sometimes find it almost impossible to ask for and accept help? Sr. Faustina sometimes had that difficulty, too, but she knew that humility means recognizing when we need help and asking for it. Toward the end of her short life, when tuberculosis was ravaging her body, Faustina experienced intense pain from the highly seasoned food served to her. Even though the pain kept her from sleeping, she did not want to ask for special food. When she mentioned her problem to her confessor, he insisted she ask for milder food. Later she wrote in her diary, "And thus I followed his directions, seeing that this humiliation was more pleasing to God."[13]

Find a quiet spot where you can relax as you meditate on Faustina's experience and how it might apply to you. Consider how accepting help when you need it is a sign of humility. Close your eyes, take a few slow, deep breaths, and then say to Jesus, "When I need help from other people, Lord, please give me the humility to ask for it from whomever you choose." If at this moment, Jesus shows you a problem in your life for which you need to seek help from another person, determine to do exactly that, no matter how much humiliation it might cause you.

❧ Throughout her years in the convent, Faustina accepted without complaint any task assigned her, no matter how lowly or dirty the job. Examine your conscience to see what daily chores, obligations, or duties you avoid—or at best do without complaining—and determine to perform them from now on to the best of your ability and without complaint.

❧ Sometimes we can have a false notion of humility, thinking that because we are sinful, weak creatures, we must despise ourselves, even hate ourselves, in order to be truly humble. But that attitude does not take into account the fact that Jesus said the second greatest commandment is to love others *as we love ourselves* (see Mark 12:31). Look honestly at your attitude toward yourself. If you discover that you do not love yourself as you should, meditate frequently on the following prayer:

For it was you who formed my inward parts;
you knit me together in my mother's womb.
I praise you, for I am fearfully and wonderfully made.
Wonderful are your works; that I know very well.
(Psalm 139:13-14)

God's Word

He has told you, O mortal, what is good;
and what does the Lord require of you
but to do justice, and to love kindness,
and to walk humbly with your God? (Micah 6:8)

Do nothing from selfish ambition or conceit, but in humility regard others as better than yourselves. (Philippians 2:3)

But this is the one to whom I will look,
to the humble and contrite in spirit,
who trembles at my word. (Isaiah 66:2)

Humble yourselves therefore under the mighty hand of God, so that he may exalt you in due time. (1 Peter 5:6)

Closing Prayer: Thank you, Lord, for convincing me of my limitations and "littleness" compared to your infinite power and majesty. Help me to not think of myself as better than anyone else. Jesus, I thank you for your loving, merciful grace, because without you I would be nothing.

1. *Diary of Saint Maria Faustina Kowalska: Divine Mercy in My Soul* (Stockbridge, MA: Marians of the Immaculate Conception, 1987), 593.
2. *Diary*, 56.
3. *Diary*, 1510.
4. *Diary*, 1510.
5. *Diary*, 593.
6. *Diary*, 493.
7. *Diary*, 270.
8. *Diary*, 93.
9. *Diary*, 1500.
10. *Diary*, 593.
11. *Diary*, 593.
12. United States Catholic Conference, *Catechism of the Catholic Church*, Second Edition (Libreria Editrice Vaticana: United States Catholic Conference, Inc., 1997), 2559.
13. *Diary*, 1429.

Meditation 13

Sharper Than Any Two-Edged Sword

Theme: In Scripture Faustina found courage, strength, resolve, and even power to thwart evil and lead a holy life. Not only did she know what God's word said, but she also internalized it, believed it, and applied it to her everyday life.

Opening Prayer: Holy Spirit, help me to read and study God's word every day so that it becomes embedded in every fiber of my heart, mind, and soul. Use that priceless wealth of Scripture to direct, strengthen, and support me in every situation in life, so that I may always avoid evil and become more and more pleasing to you.

About Faustina

Christ had entrusted to Sr. Faustina the urgent mission of writing about his divine mercy. She was to make known his longing to pour mercy upon all people—no matter how great their sins—and to give them eternal salvation. To Faustina Jesus emphasized again and again the urgent need for everyone to call on his divine mercy before his second coming (Hebrews 9:28). However, the devil, in his attempt to thwart Faustina's ongoing effort to fulfill her mission, employed a multitude of vile tricks against her. Yet he never succeeded in defeating her. Believing Scripture to be the word of God, Faustina always allowed it—along with Church tradition and authority—to guide her. Many times she used Scripture as an effective weapon against evil.

On August 12, 1934, a "mortal suffering"[1] suddenly struck Sr. Faustina, giving her a "taste of the sufferings of death."[2] So sick was she that her fellow nuns summoned her spiritual director, Msgr. Michael Sopocko, who then administered the Sacrament of the Anointing of the Sick. After the priest prayed over her, Faustina felt her health improve, so everyone left her room. But only a half hour later, she suffered another bout of sickness.

Not wanting her suffering to go to waste, Faustina thanked God for it and then united it to the sufferings of Christ crucified. In doing so, she imitated St. Paul, who said, "I am now rejoicing in my sufferings for your sake, and in my flesh I am completing what is lacking in Christ's afflictions for the sake of his body, that is, the church" (Colossians 1:24). Apparently, this positive use of her illness angered the devil, because as Faustina later revealed in her diary, "black figures full of anger and hatred"[3] for her suddenly appeared. They told her that her prayers and even her sufferings tormented them because by uniting her sufferings with those of Christ, she overpowered the evil spirits' intentions. Was Faustina afraid of those dark beings? No, because she knew Scripture was more powerful "than any two-edged sword" (Hebrews 4:12). She responded to the evil spirits with a verse from Scripture: "And the Word became flesh and lived among us" (John 1:14), and they fled "in a sudden whir."[4]

On other occasions, when harassed by evil spirits, Faustina called upon the name of Jesus, imitating the apostles who used his name to cast out demons (Acts 16:18). In fact, on one occasion in January 1937, when an evil spirit in the form of an angry "horrible cat"[5] tried to prevent Faustina from attending Mass, all she had to do was to whisper Jesus' name, and the spirit immediately vanished.

Faustina also did not hesitate to call upon her guardian angel for help when evil spirits annoyed her. She believed God's word, which says, "For he will command his angels concerning you to guard you in all your ways" (Psalm 91:11). On April 26, 1935, walking home from a religious ceremony, Sr. Faustina was halted by a "multitude of demons" who threatened her. Without hesitation, she invoked her guardian angel, and his "bright and radiant figure" told her, "Do not fear, spouse of my Lord; without His permission these spirits will do you no harm."[6] At the angel's words, the evil spirits fled.

Pause: Reflect on how Scripture supports, strengthens, and encourages you in your everyday encounters with the ungodly influences in our world.

Faustina's Words

Nothing terrifies me, even if the whole world should turn against me. All adversities touch only the surface, but they have no entry to the depths, because God, who strengthens me, who fills me, dwells there. All the snares of the enemy are crushed at His footstool.[7] (see Psalm 110:1)

Although the temptations are strong, a whole wave of doubts beats against my soul, and discouragement stands by, ready to enter into the act, the Lord, however, strengthens my will, against which all the attempts of the enemy are shattered as if against a rock.[8] (see Psalm 144)

I feel that there is a power which is defending me and protecting me from the blows of the enemy. It guards and defends me. I feel it very distinctly; it is as if I am being shielded by the shadow of His wings.[9] (see Psalm 57:1)

Reflection

Sacred Scripture was written by human authors under the inspiration of the Holy Spirit. It truly is the word of God. Scripture feeds us and gives us direction, inspiration, and strength. We can receive these benefits from Scripture through the liturgy as well as through our own reading and studying of God's word.

As Faustina did, we can treasure and venerate the wisdom of God we find in both the Old and New Testaments. Confidently we can believe with the psalmist, "Your word is a lamp to my feet and a light to my path" (Psalm 119:105). We can go forward in our daily lives, assured that God, our good shepherd, will use his word dwelling within us to always lead us in the "right paths" (Psalm 23:3).

There has never been a greater need for each of us to read, meditate on, and internalize Scripture. In these times, with ungodly influences bombarding us from every direction, we can turn to Scripture, confident that there we will find the wisdom and strength we need to live each day as "blameless and innocent children of God . . . in the midst of a crooked and perverse generation" (Philippians 2:15). With Scripture in our hearts, minds, and souls, the Holy Spirit can use God's word dwelling within us to combat the evil forces surrounding us. Scripture is indeed the living and active wisdom and power of God, "sharper than any two-edged sword, piercing until it divides soul from spirit, joints from marrow; it is able to judge the thoughts and intentions of the heart" (Hebrews 4:12).

❧ Scripture itself says that faith is a gift from God (2 Timothy 1:5-6). If you discover that you need more faith, simply ask God for it. He is a generous and loving Father on whom you can rely for all your needs in every time and every situation.

❧ What person, task, or situation in your life do you find the most trying? To deal more effectively with anyone or anything you encounter, you might first want to memorize specific Scripture verses, so that you can call them to mind when needed in any given situation. Here are a few examples of verses you might find helpful in common situations:

• When faced with a seemingly impossible task, gain strength from Philippians 4:13, just as Faustina did:[10] "I can do all things through him who strengthens me."

• When tempted with doubts and negative thinking, remind yourself that the evil one is a "liar and the father of lies" (John 8:44).

• When you have done something wrong, and it seems as if God no longer loves you and is allowing you to suffer the penalty of your actions, remind yourself that "the Lord disciplines those whom he loves" (Hebrews 12:6).

• When your heart, mind, and soul are "blinded" by sadness and depression, imitate the faith of the blind beggar Bartimaeus, who knew Jesus could restore his sight and so begged the Lord, "Jesus, Son of David, have mercy on me!" (Mark 10:47). Say this as often as you need to do so, and gradually Jesus will restore your "sight," replacing—with his light—the darkness that once blinded you.

❧ Aside from Jesus and Mary, which New Testament character do you most identify with and admire? Ask yourself why you feel a connection with this person. Open your Bible to a story involving this special person, and read it. Then meditate on this question: "Is God trying to tell me something about myself through this person?"

God does not reserve sanctity for only great saints like Faustina. He wants you, too, to become a saint. (See Jesus' exhortation to you in Matthew 5:48.) Even though the Church may never canonize you, God still wants you to one day join him in heaven, the place of eternal happiness. Do you believe this? By relying on Jesus, "the pioneer and perfecter of our faith" (Hebrews 12:2), rather than on yourself for the attainment of sanctity, you will be able to "run with perseverance the race that is set before us" (12:1). Find other Scripture passages that encourage you to desire sainthood. Pray them each day for one week, asking God to give you all the graces you need to someday dwell with him and all the saints in heaven.

God's Word

But as for you, continue in what you have learned and firmly believed, knowing from whom you learned it, and how from childhood you have known the sacred writings that are able to instruct you for salvation through faith in Christ Jesus. All scripture is inspired by God and is useful for teaching, for reproof, for correction, and for training in righteousness, so that everyone who belongs to God may be proficient, equipped for every good work. (2 Timothy 3:14-17)

Closing Prayer: My Jesus, you *are* the Word of God and the fulfillment of all Scripture. You call me to perfection. Help me to believe that by your grace I can resist evil and live a holy life as your beloved saint. As perfection itself, you have given us, Lord, the perfect prayer which I now offer to your Father and ours:

Our Father in heaven,
hallowed be your name.
Your kingdom come.
Your will be done,
on earth as it is in heaven.
Give us this day our daily bread.
And forgive us our debts,
as we also have forgiven our debtors.
And do not bring us to the time of trial,
but rescue us from the evil one. (Matthew 6:9-13)
Amen.

1. *Diary of Saint Maria Faustina Kowalska: Divine Mercy in My Soul* (Stockbridge, MA: Marians of the Immaculate Conception, 1987), 321.
2. *Diary*, 321.
3. *Diary*, 323.

4. *Diary*, 323.
5. *Diary*, 873.
6. *Diary*, 418–419.
7. *Diary*, 480.
8. *Diary*, 1086.
9. *Diary*, 1799.
10. *Diary*, 858.

MEDITATION FOURTEEN

Interior Silence

Theme: Sr. Faustina sought to maintain interior silence at all times, even when performing her assigned chores and meeting other obligations, so that she could always remain united to and communicating with the God who dwelled within her heart and soul.

Opening Prayer: Holy Spirit, sometimes it seems impossible to find quiet time in which to hear you speak to my heart. Lead me more and more deeply into the silence of your loving presence within me. Then, even when exterior silence evades me, I can, by your grace, remain in continual communication with you.

ABOUT FAUSTINA

Only two weeks after joining the Congregation of the Sisters of Our Lady of Mercy, Faustina wanted to leave. Convent life there gave her less time to silently meditate on and contemplate God than she had expected. But the Lord convinced her to stay by showing her that she could always maintain an inner silence to concentrate on his divine presence within her, no matter what assigned work she was performing and no matter what conversations and noises competed for her attention. She learned that by continually and silently acknowledging God's presence, she could, by the grace of God, remain recollected, with her heart and soul concentrating on and listening to the Lord within her.

When Sr. Faustina's assigned work schedule and other obligations allowed, she spent time in the convent chapel contemplating Jesus' real presence in the tabernacle. Before midnight Mass on Christmas Eve 1937, in spite of feeling weak and sick, she wanted to do exactly that, but instead, after sharing Christmas Eve supper with her fellow sisters, she fell asleep on her bed in her cell. Much later, when the convent bell announced that it was time to go to midnight Mass, Faustina awoke, immediately disappointed that she had slept instead of keeping the Lord company in the chapel. Still feeling sick, she hurried down to the chapel. Almost from the beginning of Mass, the Holy Spirit drew her into deep contemplation, as if graciously allowing her to make up for the time "lost" during her unintended sleep.

With the exuberant sounds of the Mass being celebrated around her, Faustina found herself steeped in the divine presence. At that moment, she received a vision of the first Christmas in Bethlehem. She saw not only the stable "filled with great radiance" but also the mother of God, who seemed "lost in the deepest of love." Faustina watched, mesmerized, as Mary tenderly wrapped her divine son in clean cloths while St. Joseph slept nearby. As Faustina gazed at the scene, Jesus' mother gently placed her newborn son in the manger, and Joseph awoke to join her in praising God. After a while, Mary and Joseph disappeared, and Faustina found herself alone with the divine infant. He stretched out his arms to her, making her realize that he wanted her to hold him. When she did, he "pressed His head against"[1] her chest and gazed upward into her eyes, letting her know how much it meant to him to be with her. Then the baby disappeared, and Faustina suddenly realized that the bell was ringing for holy Communion.

The vision had left her heart almost bursting with joy, but Faustina felt so weak and ill that she had to return to her cell before Mass ended. Nevertheless, the immense joy she experienced stayed with her throughout the entire Christmas season and helped her to remain constantly united with Jesus. Opening her heart, mind, and soul to the Holy Spirit, she prayed, "I expose my heart to the action of Your grace like a crystal exposed to the rays of the sun."[2] And the Holy Spirit honored her sincere request and kept her recollected—her heart and soul concentrating on and listening to God within her.

Pause: How often do you experience complete silence? How does it make you feel?

Faustina's Words

A distracted soul runs the risk of a fall, and let it not be surprised when it does fall. O Spirit of God, Director of the soul, wise is he whom You have trained! But for the Spirit of God to act in the soul, peace and recollection are needed.[3]

In silence I tell You everything, Lord, because the language of love is without words; not a single stirring of my heart escapes You. O Lord, the extent of Your great condescension has awakened in my soul an even greater love for You, the sole object of my love.[4]

I am trying my best for interior silence in order to be able to hear His voice. . . .[5]

Patience, prayer and silence—these are what give strength to the soul.[6]

Let Your divinity radiate through me, O You who dwell in my soul.[7]

Silent conversation, alone with You,
Is to experience what heavenly beings enjoy,
And to say to God, "I will, I will give You my heart,
 O Lord,"
While You, O great and incomprehensible One,
accept it graciously.[8]

Reflection

Even in the middle of our everyday hectic lives, when everyone and everything demand our attention and steal most opportunities for exterior silence, we can achieve interior silence in which to concentrate on God. By his grace, we can acknowledge his divine presence within our hearts.

Remaining recollected always takes effort on our part. First, we must acknowledge that recollection or contemplative prayer is a gift from God. It is something we must ask for and then put into practice, by God's grace. We need to admit that no matter how many material possessions we might have, we are still poor—poor in spirit, poor in righteousness. We must admit to God that we, like Faustina, are nothing without him. By his grace, we can then begin the lifelong process of emptying our hearts, minds, and souls of everything that is not of God, everything that is of this world—all our inner attachments to things, ideas, people, or whatever keeps us from being one with Jesus.

There are many ways in which to begin or to continue the process of turning our hearts to the Lord and seeking within ourselves the One whom our soul loves (see Song of Solomon 3:1-4). When we do, he can purify and transform us and draw us ever deeper into union with him, making us one with the triune God. Consider some of the ways presented in the exercises on the following pages.

❧ Possibly the most important way to empty ourselves of inner attachments is to seek God's forgiveness in the Sacrament of Reconciliation. There, Jesus will purify our hearts, so that he can begin to transform us into a people whose hearts are always fixed on him. When did you last receive this powerful sacrament and experience the inner healing and overwhelming peace it provides? Consider making plans to go to confession as soon as possible.

❧ Ask the Holy Spirit to help you recollect your whole being. Reading and meditating on specific Scripture passages can aid you in this process. The psalms, in particular, can help you better express yourself to God and then accept the gifts of inner communion and unity that he longs to share with you.

For instance, after asking God's Spirit to guide you, try slowly, prayerfully reading the psalm excerpts in the "God's Word" section on p. 157. Allow the first excerpt to help you accept God's invitation to commune with him in the silence of your inner being. Use the second and third excerpts to ask him to use this offering of yours to please him and to lead you into rejoicing in his presence. As you read the next two excerpts from the psalms, allow the words to become your own as you express to God your heart's great longing for him. And as you read the final excerpt, Psalm 62:5, breathe in and out slowly and deeply, relaxing every part of your body. Allow that verse to speak to your heart by repeating it as many times as needed until you reach a state of deep relaxation and "resting" in the Lord. Close your eyes, and silently acknowledge and savor God's presence deep within you. At least once a day, take time to practice this spiritual exercise.

❧ Consider meditating on the life of Christ. Prayerfully reciting the Rosary or reading the gospels can help you enter more fully into a deep communion with God. As you meditate on the life of Christ, allow the contrast between his profound humility and holiness and your own propensity toward pride and sin speak to your heart. Embrace your spiritual poverty and turn to him, acknowledging your dependence on him for your sanctification. Ask him to help you achieve an ever-deeper union with him in the silence of your heart, where you can contemplate him with the "gaze of faith."[9]

❧ In the silence of our hearts, we can hear the voice of God, even when the commotion and noise of life bombard our senses. Nevertheless, allow yourself to experience at least two minutes of complete silence each day. As you do so, close your eyes, breathe deeply and slowly, and imagine yourself held in the tender, loving arms of Jesus. Notice how you feel during as well as after these two minutes. For the next seven days, practice this exercise once a day. Each day after that period, whenever life's frenetic pace threatens to overwhelm you, recall and relive the feeling you had while resting in Jesus during these periods of silence, and trust that he is holding and supporting you even now.

❧ Depending on the season, take a walk alone through a grove of trees or a garden of flowers, or simply walk slowly over an expanse of grass. Notice how nature grows silently. In the evening, no matter the season, take a few moments alone outside to gaze up at the sky. Consider how the silent presence of the plants, trees, planets, and stars glorifies their creator. Then ponder the silence of your heart and soul, and how simply being *present* with God in that inner space can glorify him.

❧ When we allow ourselves to experience solitude, we give the Holy Spirit a perfect opportunity to speak to our hearts. During your next time alone with him, keep a pen and a journal or a sheet of paper handy. Ask God to reveal to you the reasons why in the past you have avoided solitude. Record those reasons as you ask yourself the following questions: Was I afraid I would have to face who I really am with all my shortcomings, weaknesses, and propensity toward sin? Did I doubt that God would actually speak to me? What excuses do I regularly use to avoid time alone with God? Am I just simply afraid of being alone? After writing down your answers, talk with God about them and ask him for the grace to seek out and embrace times of solitude—no matter how brief. Ask him to use these times of solitude to sanctify you and draw you ever closer to him.

❧ Slowly and meditatively read again the "Faustina's Words" section. Ask her to help you make her words your own.

GOD'S WORD

"Be still, and know that I am God!" (Psalm 46:10)

To you, O Lord, I lift up my soul. (Psalm 25:1)

May my meditation be pleasing to him,
for I rejoice in the Lord. (Psalm 104:34)

As a deer longs for flowing streams,
so my soul longs for you, O God. (Psalm 42:1)

I wait for the Lord, my soul waits,
and in his word I hope;
my soul waits for the Lord
more than those who watch for the morning,
more than those who watch for the morning.
(Psalm 130:5-6)

For God alone my soul waits in silence,
for my hope is from him. (Psalm 62:5)

Closing Prayer: Eternal, unfathomable Holy Spirit of God, I desire one thing from you: that you enlighten my mind and convince me of your loving presence deep within my heart and soul. No matter what goes on around me, no matter who or what demands my attention, keep my inner self always focused on you and communicating with you in silence. Keep me always united with you "as closely as a drop of water is united with the bottomless ocean."[10]

1. *Diary of Saint Maria Faustina Kowalska: Divine Mercy in My Soul* (Stockbridge, MA: Marians of the Immaculate Conception, 1987), 1442.
2. *Diary*, 1336.
3. *Diary*, 145.
4. *Diary*, 1489.
5. *Diary*, 1828.
6. *Diary*, 944.
7. *Diary*, 1336.
8. *Diary*, 1718.
9. United States Catholic Conference, *Catechism of the Catholic Church, Second Edition* (Libreria Editrice Vaticana: United States Catholic Conference, Inc., 1997), 2715.
10. *Diary*, 411.

Meditation Fifteen

Jesus, I Trust in You

Theme: In her diary, Faustina relates how Jesus wants each of us to place our unwavering trust in him, everywhere and at all times.

Opening Prayer: Lord, when life bombards me from every direction, I sometimes find it next to impossible to trust you to help and guide me. But St. Faustina said that distrust actually hurts you,[1] and since I do not want to hurt you, Jesus, please help me to always place my trust in you.

About Faustina

Through experience, Faustina learned that God could always be trusted, because he loved her not only like a compassionate father but also like a sweet and gentle mother. One particular way in which Jesus wanted Faustina to demonstrate her trust in him was through prayers of petition. To encourage her—and all of us—to petition God, not only for our needs, but also on behalf of others, Jesus gave us, through Faustina, a special prayer, the Divine Mercy Chaplet (see "Closing Prayer" on pp. 165–166). Along with the chaplet comes Jesus' promise that if we recite this prayer and trust him to answer, he will give us everything we ask for, as long as it is according to his will.

In particular, Jesus asked Faustina to exhort us to pray the chaplet for the dying. While praying the chaplet for dying people, Faustina discovered that Jesus would often ease a dying person's final agony and enable him or her to die in peace. Once in 1938, as Faustina entered the convent chapel, Jesus told her to pray the chaplet for a particular man who was dying. After kneeling down and beginning to pray, the young nun received a vision of the dying sinner, who was obviously being inwardly tormented by his sins. By his side, his guardian angel was trying to defend him against the attacks of a "multitude of devils,"[2] who waited to snatch the man's soul at the moment of death.

Obedient as always, Faustina continued with complete trust in God to fervently pray the Divine Mercy Chaplet for the man. As she did, Jesus appeared to her. Two rays of light flowed from his heart—just as they had appeared in the Divine Mercy image he had commanded her to have painted (see back cover). The translucent rays fell in streams of mercy onto the tormented man. Still reciting the chaplet, Faustina gazed in adoration at Jesus as the two rays of light emanating from his heart enfolded the dying man and caused the devils to suddenly vanish in fear. With the spirits of darkness gone, the man peacefully took his last breath.

Jesus told Faustina that we could obtain "everything" by praying the Divine Mercy Chaplet. So in addition to praying the chaplet for people who were dying, she also used it to petition the Lord for countless other requests. For instance, at various times she prayed the chaplet as a request for Jesus to calm violent storms,[3] to draw all people closer to God, to enable sinners to trust in his mercy, to appease God's anger,[4] to please the Lord, and to grant souls "unimaginable graces."[5] The one condition Jesus mentioned after saying he would grant us unimaginable graces was *trust*. Just as Faustina placed her trust in the Lord in all situations, so must we. With her, let us allow our minds, hearts, and souls to continually echo these words: "Jesus, I trust in you."

Pause: Consider these questions: "In what ways and situations do I exhibit trust in God? When and how do I show a lack of trust?"

Faustina's Words

When my soul is in anguish, I think only in this way: Jesus is good and full of mercy, and even if the ground were to give way under my feet, I would not cease to trust in Him.[6]

The soul gives the greatest glory to its Creator when it turns with trust to The Divine Mercy.[7]

Jesus, I trust in You! Jesus, I love You with all my heart! When times are most difficult, You are my Mother.[8]

Reflection

Jesus told Sr. Faustina to encourage us to trust in his mercy. Of course we know that the all-powerful God is ultimately in control of our lives. But in order to really trust him, we must also know how much Jesus loves each of us individually. When he appeared to Faustina as the Divine Mercy, his hands, feet, and the area above his heart manifested the wounds from his death on the cross. Contemplating his passion, we can grow in our appreciation of the infinite love with which he loves each of us. Like Faustina, we can reflect "on how much God had suffered and on how great was the love He had shown for us, and on the fact that we still do not believe that God loves us so much."[9] Thinking about all the souls she knew, Faustina wondered, "How can He convince us of His love if even His death cannot convince us?"[10]

But to truly trust God, we must also internalize the fact that no matter how many times we have sinned, no matter how unspeakable our actions, Jesus wants us to receive his mercy. In fact, he *longs* for us to abandon ourselves into his arms. There we will find only forgiveness and love because he *is* Mercy and Love. We are the lost sheep, and he is the good shepherd. When we turn to Jesus, not only when we know we need him, but even when we foolishly think do *not* need him, God rejoices. Through Faustina, Jesus says to each of us, "What joy fills My Heart when you return to me. Because you are weak, I take you in My arms and carry you to the home of My Father."[11]

May God enable us at every moment of our lives to repeat in our hearts what Jesus asked Faustina to "sign" below the image of the Divine Mercy: "Jesus, I trust in You."[12]

❧ In what situations do you find it most difficult to trust the Lord? When you are fearful of the future? When you are in physical or spiritual danger? When you have sinned and are too ashamed to turn to God? To prepare for any situation that might threaten to undermine your trust in Jesus, spend some of your prayer time each day placing yourself, those you love, and all your concerns into the loving arms of the good shepherd. You might even choose to memorize one of the most cherished of all Scriptures, Psalm 23.

❧ To help your trust in God to grow, spend time each day gazing at the image of the Divine Mercy found on the back cover. As you contemplate Jesus' image and the "signature" below it, "Jesus, I trust in You," breathe slowly and deeply. Each time you inhale, say either silently or aloud, "Jesus"; each time you exhale say, "I trust in You." As you continue to do this, consciously relax every muscle in your body, beginning with your facial muscles and slowly working your way down to your toes. When you feel completely relaxed, silence your mind and lips, close your eyes, and simply rest in Jesus, visualizing yourself tenderly held in his loving, merciful arms.

❧ When life threatens to undermine your trust in God, practice these words of St. Augustine: "Trust the past to God's mercy, the present to God's love, and the future to God's providence."[13]

❧ Distressing news and events tend to paralyze us with fear. When that happens to you, recall a recent situation in which you feared a negative outcome for yourself or those you love. Remind yourself of how everything worked out when you trusted God. Recall how the Lord strengthened and protected and cared for you. Allow those memories to fill you with renewed trust in him. You might even memorize, for future use, this Scripture verse: "We know that all things work together for good for those who love God, who are called according to his purpose" (Romans 8:28). Whenever you do recall this verse, emphasize in your mind and heart the word "everything."

As part of that "great cloud of witnesses" that always surrounds us (see Hebrews 12:1), St. Faustina can intercede for us in our needs. Consider asking her to help you trust Jesus in every situation.

❧ When you are faced with a seemingly insurmountable obstacle and anxiety threatens to overcome you, share your problem with a trusted friend, relative, priest, or other confidante as soon as possible. Ask your confidante to pray with you about the situation. In doing so, you will help to defuse your anxiety, and the prayer will help you to replace your anxiety with the love and peace of Christ.

God's Word

So we can say with confidence,
"The Lord is my helper;
I will not be afraid.
What can anyone do to me?" (Hebrews 13:6)

Trust in the Lord with all your heart,
and do not rely on your own insight. (Proverbs 3:5)

Many are the torments of the wicked,
but steadfast love surrounds those who trust in the Lord. (Psalm 32:10)

Trust in the Lord forever,
for in the Lord God
you have an everlasting rock. (Isaiah 26:4)

Closing Prayer: Using an ordinary set of rosary beads, you can fulfill Jesus' desire to pray the Divine Mercy Chaplet as follows:

First say one Our Father, one Hail Mary, and one Apostles' Creed.

On the Our Father beads, pray,

"Eternal Father, I offer you the body and blood, soul and divinity of your dearly beloved Son, our Lord Jesus Christ, in atonement for our sins and those of the whole world."

On the Hail Mary beads, pray,

"For the sake of his sorrowful passion, have mercy on us and on the whole world."

When you finish all ten decades of beads, conclude by praying three times the following: "Holy God, Holy Mighty One, Holy Immortal One, have mercy on us and on the whole world."[14]

1. *Diary of Saint Maria Faustina Kowalska: Divine Mercy in My Soul* (Stockbridge, MA: Marians of the Immaculate Conception, 1987), 50, 580.
2. *Diary*, 1565.
3. *Diary*, 1731.
4. *Diary*, 476.
5. *Diary*, 687.
6. *Diary*, 1192.
7. *Diary*, 930.
8. *Diary*, 239.
9. *Diary*, 319.
10. *Diary*, 319.
11. *Diary*, 1486.
12. *Diary*, 47.
13. Leo Knowles, *Catholic Book of Quotations* (Huntington, Indiana: Our Sunday Visitor Publishing Division, 2004), 366.
14. *Diary*, 476.

Bibliography

Bunson, Matthew. *OSV's Encyclopedia of Catholic History, Revised*. Huntington, IN: Our Sunday Visitor Publishing Division, 2004.

Dlubak, M. Nazaria, and M. Elzbieta Siepak. Translated by M. Caterina Esselen and M. Nazareta Maleta. *The Spirituality of Saint Faustina: The Road to Union with God*. Cracow, Poland: The Congregation of the Sisters of Our Lady of Mercy, 2000.

Honeygosky, Paulette G. *About My Cousin Saint Faustina*. United States: 1st Books Library, 2003.

Knowles, Leo. *Catholic Book of Quotations*. Huntington, IN: Our Sunday Visitor Publishing Division, 2004.

Kosicki, George W. *Divine Mercy's Prescription for Spiritual Health*. Huntington, IN: Our Sunday Visitor Publishing Division, 2002.

———. *John Paul II: The Great Mercy Pope*. Stockbridge, MA: John Paul II Institute of Divine Mercy, An Imprint of Marian Press, 2006.

———. *Meet Saint Faustina: Herald of Divine Mercy*. Ann Arbor, MI: Servant Publications, 2001.

———. *O Blessed Host, Have Mercy On Us!* Stockbridge, MA: Marians of the Immaculate Conception, 2000.

———. *Revelations of Divine Mercy.* Stockbridge, MA: Marians of the Immaculate Conception, 1996.

———. *Special Urgency of Mercy: Why Sister Faustina?* Steubenville, OH: Franciscan University Press, 1990.

———. *Thematic Concordance to the Diary of Saint Maria Faustina Kowalska*. Stockbridge, MA: Congregation of Marians of the Immaculate Conception, 1996.

Kosicki, George W., with David Came. *Why Mercy Sunday?* Stockbridge, MA: Marian Press, 2005.

Kosicki, George W., and Vinny Flynn. *Conversations with the Merciful God*. Stockbridge, MA: Marian Helpers, 1993.

Kowalska, Maria Faustina. *Diary of Saint Maria Faustina Kowalska: Divine Mercy in My Soul.* 3rd ed. Stockbridge, MA: Marians of the Immaculate Conception, 2001.

Michalenko, Seraphim, and Vinny Flynn. *The Divine Mercy Message and Devotion*. Stockbridge, MA: Marian Helpers, 1995.

Michalenko, Sophia. *Mercy My Mission: Life of Sister Faustina H. Kowalska, SMDM*. Stockbridge, MA: Marians of the Immaculate Conception, 1987.

Odell, Catherine M. *Faustina: Apostle of Divine Mercy*. Huntington, IN: Our Sunday Visitor Publishing Division, 1998.

Stackpole, Robert. *Jesus, Mercy Incarnate*. Stockbridge, MA: John Paul II Institute of Divine Mercy, An Imprint of Marian Press, 2000.

Stackpole, Robert, ed. *Pillars of Fire in My Soul: The Spirituality of Saint Faustina*. Stockbridge, MA: Marians of the Immaculate Conception, 2003.

Stravinskas, Peter M. J., ed. *Our Sunday Visitor's Catholic Encyclopedia, Revised Edition*. Huntington, Indiana: Our Sunday Visitor Publishing Division, 1998.

United States Catholic Conference. *Catechism of the Catholic Church, Second Edition*. United States Catholic Conference, Inc.—Libreria Editrice Vaticana, 1997.

Appendix

Divine Mercy Devotion Prayers

In her diary, Sr. Faustina recorded how Jesus requested, not only the painting of the Divine Mercy image, but also veneration of it as a "vessel"[1] for receiving God's mercy. She also recorded four other vessels of mercy Jesus requested we use:

1. Celebration of the first Sunday after Easter as the feast of Divine Mercy
2. Recitation of the Chaplet of Divine Mercy
3. Recitation of a novena of chaplets
4. Prayer every day during the Hour of Great Mercy, 3:00 p.m.—even "if only for a very brief instant"[2]—in remembrance of Christ's death on the cross

Jesus promised an abundance of graces to anyone who used these "vessels" to obtain God's mercy. All he requires of us is to trust him. "The more a soul trusts, the more it will receive."[3] And no matter how unspeakable a person's sins might be, Jesus told Faustina, he desires him or her to turn to him with trust, and he will fill them with his blessings and peace.

The Divine Mercy Chaplet: See the "Closing Prayer" in Meditation 15. pp 165–166.

Novena of Chaplets: Jesus asks us to pray a novena of Divine Mercy Chaplets on the nine days before Divine Mercy Sunday, beginning on Good Friday. To each of those nine days, Jesus assigned a special intention.

Day One: For all people, especially sinners.

Day Two: For all "priests and religious."[4]

Day Three: For "devout and faithful"[5] people.

Day Four: For all who do not believe in God and for those who do not know him.

Day Five: For "heretics and schismatics,"[6] those who have rejected the teachings of the Church and those who have formally breached union with her.

Day Six: For the souls of "little children,"[7] as well as for all people who are, like Jesus, meek and humble.

Day Seven: For all people who worship and praise God's mercy.

Day Eight: For the holy souls in purgatory.

Day Nine: For all souls who are "lukewarm"[8] in their faith.

The Hour of Great Mercy: Each day at 3:00 p.m., we are to adore and praise God's mercy; beg him to show mercy to all people, especially to sinners; and meditate on Christ's passion. We can do this by saying the Chaplet of Divine Mercy, by visiting Jesus in the nearest tabernacle, or by praying the Stations of the Cross. But if we can do none of these, Jesus said we can simply take a moment wherever we are to lift up even the briefest prayer to the Lord.

A special prayer from Jesus to say for the conversion of any sinner: "O Blood and Water, which gushed forth from the Heart of Jesus as a fount of Mercy for us, I trust in You."[9]

1. *Diary of Saint Maria Faustina Kowalska: Divine Mercy in My Soul* (Stockbridge, MA: Marians of the Immaculate Conception, 1987), 327.
2. *Diary*, 1572.
3. *Diary*, 1578.
4. *Diary*, 1212.
5. *Diary*, 1214.
6. *Diary*, 1218.
7. *Diary*, 1220.
8. *Diary*, 1228.
9. *Diary*, 187.